Sightseeing

Where is __?	Dov'è __?	doh-_veh_ __?
bridge	il ponte	_pohn_-tay
castle	il castello	kahs-_tehl_-loh
cathedral	il duomo	_dwoh_-moh
checkroom	la guardaroba	gwahr-dah-_roh_-bah
church	la chiesa	_kyay_-zah
garden	il giardino	jahr-_dee_-noh
museum	il museo	moo-_zeh_-oh
palace	il palazzo	pah-_laht_-tsoh
park	il parco	_pahr_-koh
square	la piazza	_pyaht_-tsah
ticket	il biglietto	beel-_lyayt_-toh
for two	per due	payr _doo_-ay
tourist information office	l'ufficio turistico	loof-_fee_-choh toor-_rees_-tee-koh
town center	il centro	_chehn_-troh

Days and Times

Monday	lunedì	loo-nay-_dee_
Tuesday	martedì	mahr-tay-_dee_
Wednesday	mercoledì	mayr-koh-lay-dee
Thursday	giovedì	joh-vay-_dee_
Friday	venerdì	vay-nayr-_dee_
Saturday	sabato	_sah_-bah-toh
Sunday	domenica	doh-_may_-nee-kah
minute	il minuto	mee-_noo_-toh
hour	l'ora	_oh_-rah
week	la settimana	sayt-tee-_mah_-nah
month	il mese	_may_-say

Lodging

hotel	l'albergo	ahl-_behr_-goh
pension, B&B	la pensione	payn-_syoh_-nay
reservation	la prenotazione	pray-noh-tah-_tsyoh_-nay
room	la camera	_kah_-may-rah
Do you have rooms available?	Ha camere libere?	ah _kah_-may-ray lee-bay-ray?
How much does __ cost?	Quanto costa __?	_kwahn_-toh koh-stah __?
a double room	una camera doppia	_kah_-may-rah _dohp_-pyah
a single room	una camera singola	_kah_-may-rah _seen_-goh-lah
with shower	con doccia	kohn _doht_-chah
with bath	con bagno	kohn _bahn_-nyoh
with toilet	con toilette	kohn twah-_leht_
for one night	per una notte	payr _oon_-ah _noht_-tay
for __ nights	per __ notti	payr __ _noht_-tee
from . . . to	da . . . a	dah . . . ah

Shopping

How much does it cost?		
I would like __.		
I'm looking for __.	Cerco __.	_chayr_-koh __.
Do you have?	Ha __?	ah __?
Where is __?	Dov'è __?	doh-_veh_ __?
Where are __?	Dove sono __?	doh-vay soh-noh __?
Do you take credit cards?	Prenda carte di credito?	_prehn_-dah _kahr_-tay dee _kray_-dee-toh?
that	quello/a	_kwayl_-loh/-lah
cash register	la cassa	_kahs_-sah
checkout	la cassa	_kahs_-sah
That's all.	È tutto.	eh _toot_-toh
receipt	la ricevuta	ree-chay-_voo_-tah
I'm just looking.	Sto solo guardando.	stoh _soh_-loh gwahr-_dahn_-doh
sales	saldi	_sahl_-dee
open	aperto/a	ah-_pehr_-toh/-tah
closed	chiuso/a	_kyoo_-soh/-sah
tobacconist's shop	la tabaccheria	tah-bahk-kay-_ree_-ah
bookstore	la libreria	lee-bray-_ree_-ah
market	il mercato	mayr-_kah_-toh
supermarket	il supermercato	soo-payr-mayr-_kah_-toh
department store	il grande magazzino	_grahn_-day mah-gaht-_tsee_-noh
bakery	la panetteria	pah-nayt-tay-_ree_-ah
pastry shop	la pasticceria	pahs-teet-chay-_ree_-ah
pharmacy	la farmacia	fahr-mah-_chee_-ah
hair stylist	il/la parrucchiere/a	pahr-rook-_kyeh_-ray/-rah
camera shop	il negozio di fotocine	nay-_goht_-tsyoh dee foh-toh-_chee_-nay

Colors

beige	beige	bayzh
black	nero/a	_nay_-roh/-rah
blue	blu	bloo
brown	marrone	mahr-_roh_-nay
gray	grigio/a	_gree_-joh/-jah
green	verde	_vayr_-day
pink	rosa	_roh_-sah
purple	viola	vee-_oh_-lah
red	rosso/a	_rohs_-soh/-sah
white	bianco/a	_byahn_-koh/-kah
yellow	giallo/a	_jahl_-loh/-lah
dark __	__ scuro	__ _skoo_-roh
light	__ chiaro	__ _kyah_-roh

Italian Survival Guide

The Language and Culture You Need to Travel with Confidence in Italy

Elizabeth Bingham, Ph.D.

World Prospect Press
Shell Rock, Iowa

Publisher's Note

This book is designed to help prepare travelers for their trips abroad. Its purpose is to educate and entertain. It is sold with the understanding that the publisher and author are not giving legal or financial advice. The author and World Prospect Press shall have neither liability nor responsibility to any person or entity with respect to any loss or damage caused, or alleged to be caused, directly or indirectly, by the information contained in this book.

If you do not wish to be bound by the above, you may return this book to the publisher for a full refund.

World Prospect Press
P.O. Box 100
Shell Rock, IA 50670
www.worldprospect.com

First Edition
10 9 8 7 6 5 4 3 2

Publisher's Cataloging-in-Publication
(Provided by Quality Books, Inc.)

Bingham, Elizabeth
   Italian survival guide: the language and culture you need to travel with confidence in Italy / Elizabeth Bingham. – 1st ed.
   p. cm.
   Includes bibliographical references and index.
   English and Italian.
   LCCN 2007927030
   ISBN-13: 978-0-9703734-4-1
   ISBN-10: 0-9703734-4-9
   1. Italian language—Conversation and phrase books—English. 2. Italy—Description and travel.   I. Title.

PC1121.B56 2008   458.3'421
                                   QBI07-600118

Table of Contents

In addition, I am deeply grateful to Traci Andrighetti and Sylvia Grove, who shared their skill, knowledge and passion for Italian in critiquing a late version of the manuscript. They are fine teachers and consummate editors and improved this book through their suggestions. I also thank Dr. David Birdsong, who shared his Italian contacts with me, and Antonella Olson, who served as a native-speaker reference. My work benefited immensely from all their contributions. Any errors that sneaked in are entirely my own responsibility.

Dr. Frank Donahue, although a professor of German, will recognize many of his language teaching techniques in this book. I am indebted to him for his sound, thorough and completely sensible training in foreign language pedagogy. Most recently, I benefited from the able contributions of Deborrah Langbehn and Lee Parks, who shepherded the manuscript through the printing process.

Finally, I want to thank my family for their unwavering support, despite knowing how drawn-out, demanding and financially uncertain the writing process is. Deepest appreciation goes to my husband, John, and our children, Emily and Paul, who all understand that writing duties are often more important than household duties, and who think it is normal that Mom regularly flies off to foreign lands. They are the anchors that draw me happily home from my trips.

Acknowledgments

So many people contributed to this book—people who teach Italian, people who live in Italy, people who have traveled there. Virtually everyone I approached for help was cooperative and generous and contributed greatly to the product you hold in your hands.

My first thanks go to my travel companions of yesteryear, who joined me in exploring Italy when it was a great unknown to us: Cindy Calease Weckwerth, Lynn Olson and Elaina Toenjes. With them I experienced aspects of the culture I would have missed on my own, and I benefited richly from their observations. Other visitors to Italy who shared their insights are Joe and Cherri Lock, Bruce Toenjes, David Zelle, and Eveline Ganglmair. I thank them for their contributions.

In Italy, I would like to thank Christine P. ("Blue Angel") in Rome and Bruno Serratore in Florence. They took time from their busy schedules to share native insights with a visitor, and I appreciate their kindness and aid.

I appreciate, as well, the good-humored, enthusiastic students of the beginning Italian course I taught, which formed the basis of this book. I thank in particular Joe and Cherri Lock and Liz Poole for their contributions in the classroom and out. I also thank Jan Nelson, for allowing me to teach the class and develop my approach to the language. From the student side, I would like to acknowledge Giovanni Leo, for his excellent introduction to Italian.

Many people read and commented on an early draft of this manuscript. Special thanks go to the following for their valuable, incisive critiques: Howard Mueller, Fran Mueller, Gordon Hoffert, David Zelle, Joe Lock and Cherri Lock. They each added useful points to this book, from grammar to cultural information.

About the Author

Elizabeth Bingham loves to travel and loves to teach. She combines these passions in her *Survival Guide* series, in which she prepares travelers for the language and culture they will experience abroad.

As an avid traveler, Dr. Bingham knows how useful even a little cultural knowledge and language ability are. She, too, has been in an unfamiliar country, bewildered by the foreign culture and unable to communicate. Her *Survival Guides* grew out of her desire to help others avoid that situation, to help them know what to expect, what to do, and what to say when they visit a different country. She has found that even minimal preparation can make a huge difference in the enjoyment and rewards of a trip abroad.

Dr. Bingham has a Ph.D. in Foreign Language Education/ Applied Linguistics from the University of Texas at Austin. She has taught writing and German at the university level. In addition to extensive European travel, she has lived in Germany and Austria, teaching English and conducting research there. Since 1999, she has lived in northeast Iowa, promoting foreign language and culture through teaching and writing.

Dr. Bingham can be reached through World Prospect Press at PO Box 100, Shell Rock, IA 50670, by fax at 319-885-4160 or by e-mail at bingham@worldprospect.com.

Introduction

Have you ever traveled in a country where you don't know the language? Maybe you are a little afraid of what might happen if you do. Will you get hopelessly lost? Will you not have a clue how to book a room, buy a ticket, or read a schedule? Will you order something horrible to eat because you don't know any better? And perhaps the biggest fear of all, will you make an absolute fool of yourself because you don't know any of the local customs? This is a pretty grim scenario. Almost enough to keep a would-be traveler at home. But it doesn't have to be that way!

There is a world of difference between being in a foreign country knowing nothing of the language and being in the country knowing a little of it. The first experience is confusing, frustrating and frequently misleading. (I write as one who accidently ordered two lunches for myself at the same time during my first visit to Italy, when I could not communicate beyond *yes, no, hello* and *excuse me.*)

The second experience, with just a little knowledge of the language, brims with understanding and communication, by comparison. Instead of skittering along the surface of a foreign culture, you are able to dive into it, understand some of it, and participate in it. Travel becomes a rich, heady adventure. You don't just look at museums and visit churches; you participate in the day-to-day culture of a country and its people.

Surprisingly, you don't have to devote months of time and effort to reap the benefits of a foreign language. At the start, you get huge returns for your efforts. Every little bit helps, no matter how advanced you are, but the gains are greatest at the beginning. Going from zero language knowledge to a little bit is a giant leap in ability.

You may think you don't need to know anything about a foreign language to travel in Europe, because everyone speaks English. I hate to disillusion you, but that's not exactly true. Yes, most young people now study English, and yes, people involved in tourism will usually speak at least some English, but many, many people are uncomfortable with English or simply don't know it at all. This is particularly true off the beaten path, in areas that aren't inundated with tourists, and with middle-aged and older people. While you *can* get by with English and gestures, that approach can be very frustrating. Plus, with such a language handicap, you will learn and experience a lot less of the country.

It may be especially tempting not to bother learning a new language if you will be with a guided tour group. Don't be lulled into overlooking *some* language preparation! People respond so warmly to attempts to use their language. Besides, common courtesy dictates that you should at least be able to say things like "Excuse me" and "Thank you" in a way that people in your host country will understand.

Learning a foreign language really involves learning a foreign culture, too. What good does it do to know the right words and phrases if you don't know the right time to use them? This *Survival Guide*, like any other good introduction to a foreign language, includes pertinent cultural information. Knowing about culture is important for linguistic reasons, but also for social ones—so you can fit in better, avoid offending people, and appreciate what the locals are doing. Knowing some of the culture *and* some of the language allows you to communicate more completely and have a deeper, more satisfying experience in a foreign country. And even better, the cultural information is painless to learn. As social creatures, we like to learn how people are similar to and different from ourselves.

Ideally, we would all learn a foreign language and culture before traveling abroad. You may even have bought language tapes or thought about enrolling in a course with that noble purpose in mind. Realistically, though, most of us already lead full lives, and making time for language study is not a top priority. What usually happens is that time quickly runs out, and suddenly it's a mere week before departure (or maybe even the plane flight overseas) before we get serious about tackling the language of the country

we are about to visit. That's the reality this *Survival Guide* is designed to meet. It provides the most important language and cultural
information to people with limited time to learn it.

You will learn the basics here: travel vocabulary, super-basic
grammar, everyday cultural information. All you need to add later
is a small dictionary or phrase book (for extra vocabulary) and at
least one sightseeing guide, and you're good to go. Armed with
these resources and a little training beforehand, you are sure to
have a successful visit. You can be a confident, savvy foreign
traveler, communicating with the locals, participating in daily life,
and experiencing the culture firsthand.

Please, let me know how both your studies and your trip turn out.
I would like to know what worked for you and how I can make
this book better for others. You can reach me care of World
Prospect Press, PO Box 100, Shell Rock, IA 50670 (on the Web at
www.worldprospect.com), by fax (319-885-4160), or via e-mail at
bingham@worldprospect.com.

I wish you good luck, successful studies, and happy travels!

Elizabeth

Disclaimer

Italian language and Italian culture can vary greatly from place to place and among different users in the same place. Regional, generational and socioeconomic variations remain strong to this day. While the language and culture tips offered in this book represent common usage and practices, they do not cover all the variation of speech and custom one may see in Italy. Rest assured that you can communicate with others using the material you learn from this book, even though people may pronounce words differently, have entirely different words for things, or have different local customs. Virtually all Italian speakers can understand "standard" Italian, even if that's not what they speak themselves, and you should not offend anyone if you follow the customs discussed in these pages.

1   Greetings and Introductions

Benvenuti!

Welcome to *Italian Survival Guide*, the down-to-earth, bare-bones introduction to Italian that aims to make your trip abroad as smooth and enjoyable as possible with minimal preparation. In a perfect world, all travelers would have time to take a few courses in the language of the country they are going to visit. Unfortunately, that's a reality for very few of us. Time is precious, and most language courses are long, because—let's face it—languages are complicated. That's where this *Survival Guide* comes in. It's an information-packed mini-course that concentrates on preparing you to travel in Italy in the shortest time possible. How does *Italian Survival Guide* accomplish this?

- It cuts out unnecessary vocabulary and grammar, focusing on what is most useful to you as a traveler.
- It includes important aspects of culture that you will encounter.
- It gives you lots of opportunity to practice with built-in exercises.
- It provides study tips and reality checks, so you can use your preparation time most effectively.
- It tells you what you can safely skip, if you are short on time.

This *Survival Guide* won't make you fluent in Italian. It's not magic. But it will help you communicate in the Italian language and culture. It will prepare you for what to expect as a traveler and how to deal with it, what to say and when to say it. As with any other skill, learning a foreign language does require some effort, and you get out of it what you put into it. That doesn't need to scare you off, though. Realistically, most travelers don't need to know that much of a foreign language to benefit from it. So, do what you can and enjoy your growing ability to communicate in Italian!

Absolute bare-bones Italian

Even if you acquire nothing else in Italian, do learn to say the following phrases. You will communicate on a very basic level and will earn good will for using some of the local language.

yes	sì	*see*
no	no	*noh*
please	per favore	*payr fah-voh-ray*
thank you	grazie	*graht-tsyay*
pardon me	(mi) scusi	*(mee) skoo-zee*

Study tip: Practice speaking the language as much as you can. Read aloud as you go through vocabulary lists and work on written exercises. Every bit of practice helps. When you have completed a lesson, go through it again, practicing how to say things. Try to imagine yourself in the situations described and see what you can remember to say. Try to find someone to practice *with*.

Study tip: What can you cut if you are pressed for time? The exercises, grammar tips and any vocabulary sections that you know you won't need (such as renting a car). At the very least learn greetings, manners, and some numbers, along with the simple but very useful words listed above. The culture notes are interesting and worth reading, even if you are short on time.

Study tip: If you have the time, use the exercises as a review to test what you learned earlier. Cover up any answers you wrote previously, and see whether you can do the exercises orally. If you can say your answers without too much effort at home, you will be well prepared to speak Italian abroad.

Importance of pronunciation: While you can let a lot of grammar slide and still communicate pretty well, you need a reasonably close pronunciation of words or people won't know what you are trying to say. A reasonable goal at this level is to be understandable, not necessarily to sound like a native speaker. (Surprisingly, if you sound too good, it can backfire, because native speakers may assume you know more Italian than you do and will take off at their normal high rates of speech, leaving you totally lost.) If you want to learn more about Italian pronunciation now, look over the pronunciation guide below. If you would rather get to the first vocabulary section, skip the pronunciation guide. You know it's here to come back to if you need it.

Pronunciation guide

The pronunciation guide below is just that—a guide—and is not intended to cover all possible pronunciations of letters and letter combinations in Italian. It should enable you to accurately pronounce the words in this book, however, and to take a very good stab at any new words you encounter in Italy.

Read the following tables across like this: "The Italian letter *a* is pronounced like the English sound in *father* and can be found in the words *casa* and *mangia*." American English pronunciation is used in the English examples. Try not to move your lips and tongue much when you make the vowel sounds. (Italian vowels are "purer" than American ones.)

Italian	English	Example
a	ah (f<u>a</u>ther)	c<u>a</u>sa, m<u>a</u>ng<u>ia</u>
e[1]	ay (l<u>a</u>te)	tre, s<u>e</u>ra
	eh (l<u>e</u>t)	b<u>e</u>ne, espr<u>e</u>sso
i	ee (b<u>ee</u>)	l<u>i</u>br<u>i</u>, v<u>i</u>n<u>i</u>
o	oh (t<u>o</u>ne)	m<u>o</u>lt<u>o</u>, n<u>o</u>
u	oo (c<u>oo</u>l)	t<u>u</u>tto, sc<u>u</u>si

---

[1] The most common pronunciation of the letter *e* is "ay." Sometimes, however, *e* is pronounced as "eh" if it is in the syllable that receives the most stress (=the part of the word we say most loudly), as in *bene* and *espresso* above. The pronunciations in this book show when *e* would normally be pronounced "eh," but if you prefer to pronounce every *e* as "ay" for simplicity's sake, you may certainly do so. Your pronunciation won't be perfect, but you will be perfectly understandable.

An *i* followed by another vowel is frequently contracted to make one syllable starting with a "y" sound. You can get this same sound by pronouncing each vowel separately but very quickly.

ia	yah (<u>ya</u>da)	p<u>ia</u>tti, dopp<u>ia</u>
ie	yay (<u>ye</u>a)	graz<u>ie</u>, v<u>ie</u>ne
io	yoh (<u>yo</u>yo)	ol<u>io</u>, pens<u>io</u>ne
iu	yoo (<u>you</u>)	a<u>iu</u>tare, p<u>iù</u>

When they are in certain combinations, a number of consonants in Italian are pronounced differently than we would expect. In particular, you will see that *c*, *ch*, *g*, *gh* and *sc* are all pronounced "differently" when they are followed by *e* or *i*. There are other surprises, as well, as you will see below. These unexpected pronunciations include the following.

ci	ch or chee (<u>ch</u>ow or <u>chee</u>se)	<u>ci</u>ao, arriveder<u>ci</u>
ce	chay (<u>cha</u>se)	pia<u>ce</u>re, <u>ce</u>na
chi	kee (<u>key</u>)	zuc<u>chi</u>ni, <u>Chi</u>anti
che	kay (<u>ca</u>ble)	per<u>ché</u>, mac<u>che</u>roni
gi	j or jee (<u>J</u>oe or <u>jee</u>p)	<u>gi</u>orno, <u>gi</u>ta
ge	jay (blue <u>jay</u>)	<u>ge</u>lato, <u>ge</u>neroso
gh	g (<u>g</u>irl)	spa<u>gh</u>etti, <u>gh</u>etto
gli	lly (mi<u>lli</u>on)	fi<u>gli</u>a, consi<u>gli</u>are
gn	ny (ca<u>ny</u>on)	lasa<u>gn</u>e, <u>gn</u>occhi
qu	kw (<u>qu</u>ick)	<u>qu</u>ando, ac<u>qu</u>a
sce	shay (<u>sha</u>me)	pe<u>sce</u>, <u>sce</u>ndere
sci	sh or she (<u>sh</u>arp or <u>she</u>ep)	<u>sci</u>arpa, u<u>sci</u>ta
z, zz	ts (ca<u>ts</u>)	pi<u>zz</u>a, gra<u>z</u>ie
	ds (be<u>ds</u>)	<u>z</u>ero, <u>z</u>abaglione

Be aware that many consonants are "doubled" in Italian. If you see, for example, *tt*, as in *spaghetti*, the *t* sound should be held longer than you would normally say it. Also, *h* is always silent in Italian, as in the English words *honest* and *honor*.

Finally, a word of warning about the American *r*. It is much harder and flatter than the *r* in Italian. The Italian *r* is more like a trill. When you speak Italian, try to trill your *r*. If you can't, at least try to soften it (make it sound like the *r* in a British accent, as in "muth-uh" for *mother*).

Culture note—Giovanni and Giorgio

Many English speakers do their best to pronounce Italian words and names the way an Italian would, but some pronunciations are less obvious because certain letter combinations can mislead learners of the language. For example, the combination "gi" is often pronounced "jee," as in *gita* (trip) or Gina (girl's name). That works fine when the *i* is the only vowel in the syllable. But when the "gi" precedes another vowel in the same syllable, such as in *giorno* (day), then it leads to just the "j" sound, "<u>johr</u>-noh," in this case. You can see the same pattern with "ci"—on its own in a syllable (*arrivederci* or *cinema*), it is pronounced "chee," but in front of another vowel in the same syllable, it's just "ch" (*ciao* is "chow," not "chee-ow").

Two names that are commonly mispronounced by learners of Italian are Giovanni and Giorgio, and you can see why now. Careful learners see the "gi" at the start, dutifully say "jee" followed by the rest of the name, and end up with an extra syllable or two. In both these cases, "gi" = "j". Giovanni is pronounced "joh-<u>vahn</u>-nee" and Giorgio is pronounced "<u>johr</u>-joh." Just think of "Joe" and "George." Our English versions are closer to the correct Italian than the "jee-oh" versions are.

Exercise 1.1

Match each group of letters to the correct pronunciation.

1.	co	A.	*koo*
2.	ci	B.	*koh*
3.	ce	C.	*chay*
4.	ca	D.	*kah*
5.	cu	E.	*chee*

Answers: 1) B, 2) E, 3) C, 4) D, 5) A

1.	ci	A.	*kee*
2.	chi	B.	*chee*
3.	ce	C.	*kay*
4.	che	D.	*chay*

Answers: 1) B, 2) A, 3) D, 4) C

1.	ga	A.	*jay*
2.	ge	B.	*goh*
3.	gi	C.	*jee*
4.	go	D.	*goo*
5.	gu	E.	*gah*

Answers: 1) E, 2) A, 3) C, 4) B, 5) D

1.	ge	A.	*jee*
2.	ghe	B.	*gay*
3.	gi	C.	*gee*
4.	ghi	D.	*jay*

Answers: 1) D, 2) B, 3) A, 4) C

1.	ia	A.	*kwah*
2.	io	B.	*yoh*
3.	gli	C.	*nyah*
4.	ghi	D.	*lly*
5.	gna	E.	*yah*
6.	qua	F.	*gee*

Answers: 1) E, 2) B, 3) D, 4) F, 5) C, 6) A

1.	ci	A.	*chee*
2.	sci	B.	*shay*
3.	ce	C.	*kay*
4.	sce	D.	*kee*
5.	che	E.	*shee*
6.	chi	F.	*chay*

Answers: 1) A, 2) E, 3) F, 4) B, 5) C, 6) D

Reality check: If you are afraid that you must be semi-fluent in Italian to travel to Italy, don't be. You can get by quite well in tourist spots with no Italian whatsoever. Most workers in the tourist industry will know at least some English.

On the other hand, if you think there is no real need to learn any Italian, realize that many Italians do not speak English or speak only minimal English, even in highly touristed areas. When you get away from the tourist centers, a little Italian can make your life much easier. In addition, you earn great good will when you try to use Italian. Italians will appreciate your attempts to use their language. They may find you amusing, as well, which leads to warmer interactions and more help.

Culture note—Variations in greetings

The most appropriate greeting in Italy varies according to time of day and location. For example, in Tuscany you will frequently hear *ciao* even in formal greetings, but in Rome you may hear *buon giorno* almost exclusively. *Buon giorno* can safely carry you to late afternoon or dusk in most parts of the country; then people will start using *buona sera*. In some places, however, *buona sera* can also be used after 2 p.m. to mean "good afternoon" or "goodbye." Confusing? The wisest course of action is to listen to what locals say (particularly when addressing *you*) and use that form.

Greetings

A good place to start when learning a new language is with greetings. If you can say hello to people, they are likely to think you are friendly and will think well of you, even if you can't say anything else in their language.

Hi! (informal)	Ciao!	*chow*
Good morning!	Buon giorno!	*bwohn johr-noh*
Good day!	Buon giorno!	*bwohn johr-noh*
Good evening!	Buona sera!	*bwohn-ah say-rah*

Culture note—Physical closeness

You will quickly notice that Italians are much more physically demonstrative than most Americans are. Greetings between Italians usually involve kisses or handshakes, as do departures. Friends and family members hold hands or link arms when they are out together, even men, in some parts of the country. People stand more closely to each other. (It's not an invasion of personal space.) They may even stroke each other's cheek or pat their arm or back in affection as they talk.

Culture note—Kiss or shake hands?

Italians usually have some physical contact when they greet or part from each other. Relatives and long acquaintances—including men meeting other men—usually kiss both cheeks (right, then left), often gripping their right hands. When they are not relatives or close friends, men generally shake each others' hands when meeting or departing, often grabbing the other man's arm with the free hand. Women may shake a man's hand or kiss his cheek.

What should tourists do? Unless you are visiting relatives who envelope you in hugs and and cover you with kisses, it's safest to begin with (and probably stick with) a handshake. You should use a firm grip when shaking hands and maintain direct eye contact.

Culture note—The Latin lover

Gallantry is deeply engrained in Italian society, with men holding doors for women, kissing their hands and openly admiring attractive females, often verbally. Foreign women—particularly blondes—are frequently hit on by local men. Most of the advances are harmless (if hopeful) flirtation. If you are verbally harrassed, the best response is usually none at all. If you get fed up, you could say, "Vai via!" [vah-ee vee-ah] (Go away!). To avoid unwanted attention, you should dress conservatively and try not to look like a tourist. Conversely, if you are a female looking for romance in Italy, there's a good chance you can find it.

Introductions

One of the joys of travel is meeting new people. Learn how to introduce yourself and ask others their names.

(Lit.) How do you call yourself?	Come si chiama?	*koh-may see kyah-mah?*
I call myself ___.	Mi chiamo ___.	*mee kyah-moh __*
Pleased to meet you.	Piacere!	*pyah-chay-ray*
And you?	E Lei?	*ay leh-ee?*
How are you?	Come sta?	*koh-may stah?*
(I'm) fine, thanks.	(Sto) bene, grazie.	*(stoh) beh-nay, graht-tsyay*

Culture note—Names

When identifying themselves, Italians often give their last name first, for example, "Martini Laura." Young people, however, might introduce themselves by their first names, as will family members. Try to follow the lead of others when introducing yourself.

Culture note—Formality

The Italian language, like many others, preserves a distinction in formality that the English language has long since dropped. There is a formal way to address people, the *Lei* ("leh-ee") form, as well as an informal way, the *tu* ("too") form. Italian speakers usually address people they don't know well or whom they know in formal contexts with the formal *Lei* form. Addressing someone with the wrong level of formality could cause offense, particularly if you are too informal. Because travelers interact primarily if not exclusively with strangers, this guide discusses just the *Lei* form.

Do note, however, that family members, intimate friends and young people use the *tu* form with each other. Thus, if you visit Italian relatives, they will probably use the *tu* form with you, even though you may never have met them before.

Culture note—Prestige and respect

Italians are very conscious of prestige and the need to show respect. Courtesy dictates that the person with less prestige is introduced to the person of greater prestige as a way of showing respect. So to be polite, men should be introduced to women, the young to the old, before the reverse. The person of higher prestige should also extend a hand first.

Culture note—Titles

Italians love to use titles. You will frequently hear the words for mister (*signore*), missus or madam (*signora*) or miss (*signorina*), with or without the last name. In a business situation, a woman is usually called a *signora*, regardless of her marital status.

In addition, all who graduate from a university may call themselves doctor (*dottore* for men, *dottoressa* for women). High school and university teachers are called professor (*professore/professoressa*), and engineers are *ingegnere*. There are many other titles that you might hear, including courtesy titles that don't really indicate much at all but sound good.

Study tip: Do the exercises if you have time to. If you don't have time, skip them. They help, but you can get by with oral practice.

Exercise 1.2

Can you get through an Italian introduction without looking at the answers? How do you say the following in Italian?

1. My name is _____.

2. What's your name?

3. How are you?

4. Fine, thanks.

Answers: 1) Mi chiamo ___. 2) Come si chiama? 3) Come sta? 4) (Sto) Bene, grazie.

A word about grammar

Knowing a little bit of grammar can make using a language easier, because you can see some of the language's underlying system, the order, the rules for how things work. This book presents small "bites" of grammar throughout. If you find them interesting or useful, great! Follow the rules and make your Italian more grammatically accurate. If you find grammar to be boring or confusing, skip the grammar sections. Grammaticality is the frosting on the foreign language cake. It makes things "look" nice, "taste" a little sweeter, but the main component of communication (the "cake," so to speak) is vocabulary. Ideally you will learn vocabulary and grammar hand in hand, but if you have limited time and have to choose between grammar and vocabulary, definitely concentrate on vocabulary. You will get a lot more bang for your buck there.

Grammar—Verb endings (present tense)

parl<u>are</u> (to speak), ved<u>ere</u> (to see), part<u>ire</u> (to leave)

Subject	Verb ending	Example
io (I)	-o	parl<u>o</u>, ved<u>o</u>, part<u>o</u>
Lei (you)	-a/-e	parl<u>a</u>, ved<u>e</u>, part<u>e</u>

Verbs are usually listed in language books and dictionaries in the *infinitive* form. The infinitive form is the basic form of the verb, the form it is in before we start changing it to reflect who or what is doing the action (changing the verb like this is called *inflecting* the verb). In English, the infinitive form of a verb uses the word *to* followed by the verb, for example, *to be*. That is why translations of Italian verbs are usually listed after *to*, to indicate that the verbs are in their basic, infinitive state.

When we *inflect* the verb, we change it to show who or what is doing the action. The English verb forms *is, am* and *are* are all inflected forms of the verb *to be*. In English (or whatever your native language is) you automatically know how to inflect the verb for person (*I* versus *you* versus *she*) and for number (singular or plural). Even though the inflection is automatic, it still follows rules of the language that you internalized as a child and don't have to think about. When we learn a foreign language, most of us have to think about the rules, at least until we get enough experience that they become automatic, too. Here are the rules for inflecting most Italian verbs (summarized in the table above).

The verb in infinitive form consists of two parts, the stem and an ending of *-are*, *-ere* or *-ire*. For example, here are some verbs that you will see in this book, with a hyphen added to separate the stem from the ending: *parl-are* (to speak), *chiam-are* (to call), *ripet-ere* (to repeat), *ved-ere* (to see), *part-ire* (to depart), *dorm-ire* (to sleep).

With most verbs, you start with the stem of the verb, for example *parl-*, and add to it to show who the verb refers to. If you want to talk about yourself, you will add the ending *-o* to the verb stem: *(io) parlo* (I speak). If you are talking directly to someone (usually using a question or command), you need to know whether the verb has an *-are* ending or not. If the verb ends in *-are*, you add an *-a* to the verb stem: *(Lei) parla* (You speak), or, more likely for us, *Parla (Lei) . . .?* (Do you speak. . .?). For verbs that end in *-ere* or *-ire*, you add an *-e* to the verb stem: *Vede (Lei)?* (Do you see?) or *Parte (Lei)?* (Are you leaving?).

Reality check: If this concern with the "kind of verb" (whether it ends in *-are*, *-ere* or *-ire*) for the *Lei* form seems confusing, take heart. You really don't need to speak directly to people (using the "you" form) much as a traveler, and when you do, you will usually want just a few forms that you have practiced a lot.

Grammar—Pronouns

Note that the examples above show the words for *I* (*io*) and *you* (*Lei*) in parentheses. That is because those words are usually not used; they are left out. The ending of the verb usually shows who is being talked about. An *-o* ending means the speaker is being talked about, and an *-a* or *-e* ending means the listener. This is one of the trade-offs of language. Italians verb forms are more complicated than English, but they convey more information and can make other parts of the sentence simpler because of that. You *can* include the *I* or the *you* in your sentence, but Italians usually save that for clarity or for emphasis.

Culture note—The gracious guest

Italians do not often invite new acquaintances into their homes. It's an honor if you are invited to someone's house or apartment. You should arrive about ten minutes later than the agreed-upon time and bring a small gift for your hosts, such as flowers or candy. Bear in mind that Italians value quality over quantity, so something small but a little more expensive would be appropriate as a hostess gift. In some homes, you will be asked to remove your shoes. Your hosts may offer you house slippers to wear during your stay.

Grammar—Forming questions

The easiest way to form questions in Italian is to use the same form you would for a statement, but raise your voice at the end to sound questioning (called "rising intonation"). For example, say you can't quite read the price on an item you would like to buy. You could ask "Costa 30 euro?" for confirmation. The vendor could emphatically correct you using the same form as a statement: "No. Costa *80* euro."

Another way to ask questions is to start with a question word or phrase, such as "how" or "from where," and follow it with the verb. "Come sta?" (How are you?) "Da dove viene?" (Where do you come from?) "Quanto costa?" (How much does it cost?) If you want to ask a longer question, you can add more information after the verb: "Quanto costa una camera doppia con bagno per tre notti?" (How much does a double room with bath for three nights cost?).

A third way to ask questions is to use inverted word order, switching the subject of the sentence and the predicate

(everything after the subject, most importantly the verb), such as
"È incluso il servizio?" (Is service included?). This version takes a
little more thought, so beginners may want to stick with the
perfectly acceptable variations above.

Exercise 1.3

Practice inflecting the regular verbs below. *Regular* means that the
verbs follow the rules as we expect them to.

1. ordinare (*to order*)

    I order/you order

2. pagare (*to pay*)

    I pay/you pay

3. chiamare (*to call*)

    I call/you call

4. aiutare (*to help*)

    I help/you help

5. parlare (*to speak*)

    I speak/Do you speak?

6. partire (*to depart/leave*)

    I leave/you leave

7. cercare (*to look for*)

    I'm looking for/Are you looking for?

8. consigliare (*to recommend*)

    I recommend/Do you recommend?

9. ripetere (*to repeat*)

    I repeat /you repeat

Anwers: 1) (io) ordino/(Lei) ordina, 2) (io) pago/(Lei) paga, 3) (io) chiamo/(Lei) chiama,
4) (io) aiuto/(Lei) aiuta, 5) (io) parlo/(Lei) parla, 6) (io) parto/(Lei) parte, 7) (io)
cerco/(Lei) cerca?, 8) (io) consiglio/(Lei) consiglia?, 9) (io) ripeto/(Lei) ripete

---

Culture note—Gestures

Gestures are extremely important in Italy, not only gestures of affection, but gestures that convey particular meanings.

If someone sweeps their hand in a snatching motion in front of them (usually accompanied by a whistling noise), they are warning of pickpockets. If they brush their hand out away from under their chin, it means, "I couldn't care less." Pulling the lower lid of the eye down means, "Watch out" or "evil eye" (as a joke). Screwing the end of the index finger into the cheek means something is good or delicious.

Some gestures you will want to avoid are tapping your head with your index finger (you are calling someone crazy) and the OK symbol (considered vulgar, representing a body part). The money symbol (rubbing the thumb and fingers together) is all right.

Grammar—Irregular verbs

Just when you thought verbs were confusing enough, along comes a large group of *irregular* verbs that don't follow the usual rules. Many of the most common verbs are irregular. For example, one big exception to the verb inflection rules is the verb *to be*, which is highly irregular in all western European languages, including English. In Italian, the infinitive form of *to be* is *essere*, but the inflected forms are *(io) sono* and *(Lei) è*. You have to memorize irregular forms. Here are some very common irregular verbs.

to be	to have	to come	to go
essere	*avere*	*venire*	*andare*
(io) sono	(io) ho	(io) vengo	(io) vado
(Lei) è	(Lei) ha	(Lei) viene	(Lei) va

Study tip: If your goal is to learn more Italian in the future, to be as proficient as possible, you should be as accurate as you can. Read and use the grammar tips, pay attention to your verb endings, and learn the gender of nouns (we will get to this in Chapter Two).

Culture note—Geographical differences

Italy is split culturally and economically between north and south, with the division running roughly through Rome.

The north is more industrialized, modernized, productive and prosperous. The south has a milder climate, a slower pace of life and is traditionally agrarian. It is also poorer, less progressive, and suffers from higher unemployment, more crime, and more political upheaval than the north. The farther south you go, the fewer people will speak English.

Many tourists are more comfortable in modern, wealthy northern Italy. Others find that southern Italy best embodies the zest and exhuberance of the Italian spirit.

Origins

It seems that people always want to know where travelers are from. Be prepared to recognize the following questions and know how to answer them.

from	da	*dah*
where	dove	*doh-vay*
where from?	da dove?	*dah doh-vay?*
Where do you come from?	Da dove viene?	*dah doh-vay vyay-nay?*
I come from	Vengo da	*vayn-goh dah*
from the U.S.	dagli Stati Uniti	*dah-lyee stah-tee oo-nee-tee*
And you?	E Lei?	*ay leh-ee?*

Some country names

Italy	Italia	*ee-tahl-yah*
England	Inghilterra	*een-geel-teh-rah*
the United States	gli Stati Uniti	*lyee stah-tee oo-nee-tee*
Canada	Canada	*kah-nah-dah*

Germany	Germania	*jayr-<u>mahn</u>-yah*
Austria	Austria	*<u>ow</u>-stree-ah*
Switzerland	Svizzera	*<u>zveet</u>-tsay-rah*
France	Francia	*<u>frahn</u>-chah*
Spain	Spagna	*<u>spahn</u>-nyah*

Directional phrases

north of	al nord da	*ahl <u>nord</u> dah*
south of	al sud da	*ahl <u>sood</u> dah*
east of	all'est da	*ahl-<u>ehst</u> dah*
west of	all'ovest da	*ahl-<u>oh</u>-vayst dah*
close to	vicino a	*vee-<u>chee</u>-noh ah*

Culture note—Origins

If you hail from the United States, your country is properly called *gli Stati Uniti* in Italian, although many Italians will refer to it simply as *l'America*. Regardless of local preference, you may identify yourself as an American (*americano/-a*) without fear of confusion with the rest of the Americas.

Unless you live in a large and well-known city (New York, Chicago, Miami, Los Angeles) or in a well-known state (New York, Florida, California), most people won't recognize the place name or know where it is. To give them an idea, tell where your home is in relation to a place people might know.

Exercise 1.4

Practice asking and telling about origin.

1. Ask someone where she is from.

2. Tell where you are from.

3. Describe where that is.

Answers: 1) Da dove viene? 2) Vengo ____. 3) varies

Leave-taking

Just as you will want to say hello to people, you will want to say goodbye.

goodbye	arrivederci!	*ah-reev-ay-<u>dayr</u>-chee*
'bye (informal)	ciao!	*chow*
goodnight	buona notte!	*<u>bwohn</u>-ah <u>noht</u>-tay*

Culture note—How not to look like a tourist

It's unlikely that you will blend so well into Italian society that no one will identify you as a foreigner, but you can minimize the fact that you are a tourist.

Why does it matter? For one thing, people appreciate it when visitors care enough to learn about their customs and try to fit in. You will probably get a warmer reception from locals. For another reason, obvious tourists are sitting ducks for petty criminals, who abound in certain urban areas. The more American you look, the more people will think you are "easy pickings." A third reason to care is that U.S. foreign policy sometimes leads to anti-American sentiment abroad. No one is likely to say or do anything to you, but why draw attention to yourself?

If you follow these easy guidelines, you will stand out much less as an American in Italy:

—don't wear white tennis shoes
—don't wear a ball cap
—don't wear blue jeans or especially track suits
—don't wear a fanny pack
—don't talk too loudly
—don't wear a lot of makeup
—don't hang a camera around your neck
—*do* attempt to use Italian

Culture note—The departing kiss

In keeping with the greater formality and physicality of Italian society, most people kiss cheeks or shake hands upon departing. This is unlikely to affect you as a tourist, however.

Manners

It always pays to be polite when you are traveling in a foreign country. Learning how to say *please, thank you* and *excuse me* should be a top priority.

Please.	Per favore.	*payr fah-voh-ray*
	Per piacere.	*payr pyah-chay-ray*
Thank you (very much).	(Mille) grazie.	*(meel-lay) graht-tsyay*
You're welcome.	Prego.	*preh-goh*
Excuse me.	(Mi) scusi.	*(mee) skoo-zee*
May I get past?	Permesso?	*payr-mays-soh?*
I'm sorry.	Mi dispiace.	*mee dees-pyah-chay*
That's OK.	Va bene.	*vah beh-nay*

Culture note—La bella figura

Good manners are particularly important in Italy, for they form a large part of the overall impression you make—your *figura*. A good image (*bella figura*) is highly prized and continually aimed for.

The *bella figura* is based on appearance (being well groomed, fashionable and elegant), on attitude (projecting confidence and self-importance) and on behavior (showing proper respect and manners). If you are impolite, sloppily dressed or otherwise conduct yourself poorly, you will have a *brutta figura* (bad image), to be avoided at all costs.

Exercise 1.5

What might you say in each of these situations?

1. Someone thanks you.

2. You bump into someone slightly.

3. You bump into someone hard.

4. You're making a request.

5. Someone has given you something.

6. You'd like to make your way through a crowd.

7. Someone apologizes to you for something minor.

A. Per favore./Per piacere.

B. Mi dispiace.

C. Grazie.

D. Permesso?

E. Mi scusi.

F. Prego.

G. Va bene.

Answers: 1) F, 2) E, 3) B, 4) A, 5) C, 6) D, 7) G

Culture note—Small-talk taboos

Certain topics should be avoided with people you don't know well. Bringing up any of the following will quickly tarnish your image: the Mafia, politics, religion, taxes, WWII. You should also avoid asking people what they do for a living, unless they bring it up first. And don't complain to Italians about Italy.

Ignoring these taboos will be considered ill-mannered or even insulting. Remember, Italians prize diplomacy, so try to curb your curiosity. (Back to *la bella figura*.) And whatever you talk about, don't do it too loudly. Italians may speak loudly among themselves, but to them a loud tourist really stands out in a negative way.

Useful Expressions

yes	sì	*see*
no	no	*noh*
maybe	forse	*fohr-say*
and	e	*ay*
or	o	*oh*
but	ma	*mah*
Just a moment.	un momento	*oon moh-mayn-toh*
Right away.	subito	*soo-bee-toh*
I don't understand.	Non capisco.	*nohn kah-pees-koh*
Can you___?	Può ___?	*pwoh ___?*
to repeat	ripetere	*ree-peh-tay-ray*
Can you repeat?	Può ripetere?	*pwoh ree-peh-tay-ray?*
to speak	parlare	*pahr-lah-ray*
slowly	lentamente	*layn-tah-mayn-tay*
Can you speak slowly?	Può parlare lentamente?	*pwoh pahr-lah-ray layn-tah-mayn-tay?*
more	più	*pyoo*
More slowly, please?	Più lentamente, per favore?	*pyoo layn-tah-mayn-tay, payr fah-voh-ray?*
more loudly	più forte	*pyoo fohr-tay*

Exercise 1.6

Write what you would say in each of these situations.

1. Someone is speaking too quickly.

2. You would like something repeated.

3. Someone is speaking too softly.

4. You don't understand.

5. You need a few seconds to complete something.

Answers: 1) (Può parlare) più lentamente? 2) Può ripetere? 3) (Può parlare) più forte? 4) Non capisco. 5) Un momento.

Culture note—Business cards

Italians often give calling cards or business cards when meeting people. This is a way of showing their education and job title (which indicate their social status) without bringing up the touchy subject of their occupation among people they do not know well. Feel free to use such cards when you introduce yourself.

2   Lodging

Numbers (0-10)

Numbers are among the most useful vocabulary items you will learn in a foreign language. Learning all the numbers at once can be an overwhelming task, so this book breaks numbers into five different lessons. Start at the beginning and learn to count from zero to ten.

0	zero	*dzeh-roh*
1	uno	*oo-noh*
2	due	*doo-ay*
3	tre	*tray*
4	quattro	*kwaht-troh*
5	cinque	*cheen-kway*
6	sei	*seh-ee*
7	sette	*seht-tay*
8	otto	*oht-toh*
9	nove	*noh-vay*
10	dieci	*dyeh-chee*

Culture note—Handwritten numbers

Italian numbers can be a little confusing when written by hand. *Ones* have a swoop leading up to them, so they often look like *sevens* to American eyes. Italians don't confuse them with *sevens*, though, because *sevens* have little bars crossing their stems. You will encounter handwritten numbers on bills, on some price tags, and on restaurant specials that are listed on blackboards.

Exercise 2.1
After practicing the numbers to yourself, translate the following into Italian.

1. zero

2. six

3. one

4. seven

5. two

6. eight

7. three

8. nine

9. four

10. ten

11. five

1) zero, 2) sei, 3) uno, 4) sette, 5) due, 6) otto, 7) tre, 8) nove, 9) quattro, 10) dieci, 11) cinque

---

Culture note—Counting on fingers

When Italians count on their fingers, they start with their thumbs. Thus, a count of *one* is indicated by sticking one thumb out. *Two* is the thumb and forefinger, etc. *Six* is all five fingers on one hand and the thumb on the other hand. It's useful to know this before ordering something at a bar or bakery or anywhere else you might indicate number by holding up fingers. For example, in a crowded bar, you could accidentally double your order if you hold your index finger up, American style, to order one sandwich. When the worker sees that you have the index finger up, he could assume that the thumb is out, too, and bring you two sandwiches.

Exercise 2.2
Practice some simple math.

1. quattro più (plus) tre =

2. cinque meno (minus) tre =

3. sei più quattro =

4. nove più zero =

5. otto meno uno meno sette =

6. sei meno cinque =

7. uno più tre =

8. dieci meno quattro =

9. nove meno sei =

10. cinque più tre =

11. quattro più uno =

Answers: 1) sette, 2) due, 3) dieci, 4) nove, 5) zero, 6) uno, 7) quattro, 8) sei, 9) tre, 10) otto, 11) cinque

Travel tip: When planning a trip to Italy, you may want to consider staying in a rural area, perhaps with an Italian family. The Internet is invaluable in showing you what rural housing is available and allowing you to book a place in advance. A villa in the Tuscan countryside? A cottage in the mountains? You can read about specific rentals online by searching on the keyword "agriturismo," which will lead you to Internet sites such as www.agriturismo.it.

Grammar—Gender of nouns

-o ending	-a ending	-e ending
masculine	feminine	either
giorno (day)	tavola (table)	madre (mother)
libro (book)	lampada (lamp)	padre (father)

In Italian, all nouns have a "gender." Every noun is either masculine or feminine. This is an example of *grammatical gender*, where gender has everything to do with grammar and less to do with natural or biological sex. While nouns for people and animals usually follow natural gender (nouns for males are masculine and nouns for females are feminine), things are less clear for nouns that *don't* refer to people or animals. For example, in Italian, a wall is masculine (*il muro*), but a room is feminine (*la camera*). A book is masculine (*il libro*), but its paper is feminine (*la carta*). Often there is no clear connection between the gender of a noun and the real world. ("Egg," for example, is masculine—*l'uovo*.) Fortunately, the words themselves give us clues as to their gender. (See the table above.) Nouns that end in *-o* are masculine. Nouns that end in *-a* are feminine. The main identity problem is with nouns that end in *-e*, because they could be either masculine or feminine.

It's a good idea to learn the gender of a noun along with the noun itself. That's why vocabulary listings in course books and dictionaries include an indication of the noun's gender: *il* or *m* for masculine, and *la* or *f* for feminine. The bad news is that grammatical gender can be hard to keep straight. The good news is that using the wrong gender with a noun will hardly ever keep people from understanding you.

Exercise 2.3
Identify the following nouns as masculine or feminine based on their endings or meanings.

1. madre (mother)
2. tavola (table)
3. zio (uncle)
4. zia (aunt)
5. camera (room)
6. libro (book)
7. padre (father)
8. ora (hour)
9. letto (bed)
10. porta (door)
11. minuto (minute)
12. ricevuta (receipt)

Answers: 1) F, 2) F, 3) M, 4) F, 5) F, 6) M, 7) M, 8) F, 9) M, 10) F, 11) M, 12) F

Grammar—Definite articles, singular

before a . . .	Masculine *the*	Feminine *the*
consonant	**il** bagno (the bath) **il** letto (the bed)	**la** camera (the room) **la** madre (the mother)
vowel	**l'**albergo (the hotel) **l'**acquaio (the sink)	**l'**ora (the hour) **l'**amica (the female friend)
z or s + consonant	**lo** zio (the uncle) **lo** stadio (the stadium)	**la** zia (the aunt) **la** stazione (the station)

As you may know, the word *the* is called a *definite article*, because it usually refers to some definite noun—*the* table, *the* book, *the* jacket. The definite article changes in Italian according to the gender of the noun and what letter the noun starts with. If a noun is masculine, *the* must also be masculine. It should also "fit" with the first letter of the noun. For example, if the noun begins with a consonant, the masculine form of *the* is *il* (as in *il bagno*, the bath). If the masculine noun begins with a vowel, then *the* is expressed as *l'* (as in *l'albergo*, the hotel). If the masculine noun begins with a *z* or an *s+consonant*, then *the* is expressed as *lo* (as in *lo zio*, the uncle).

Things are slightly simpler with feminine nouns. If the feminine noun begins with a consonant, *the* is expressed as *la* (as in *la camera*, the room). If the feminine noun begins with a vowel, then *the* is shortened to *l'* (as in *l'ora*, the hour).

🔥 **Survival Strategy:** If you want to simplify your Italian and worry about only one form of *the* for masculine nouns, use *il*. To focus on just one feminine form, use *la*. The odds are in your favor that you will be correct. You still have the challenge of identifying which nouns are feminine and which are masculine, though. To simplify even further, you could use *la* for all nouns that end in *-a* and *il* for everything else (except words that you know are feminine, such as *madre*). They won't be the right choices all the time, but they will probably be understood.

💣＊   **Simplified gender and definite articles**

Noun ending	Good-guess gender	Good-guess def. article (the)
-a	feminine	la
-o or -e (except obviously feminine words, like *madre*)	masculine	il

Note: Using this shortcut will result in some ungrammatical forms. They should still be understandable, though.

Exercise 2.4
Supply the correct form of *the* for the following nouns. The gender of the noun is indicated after the word itself by M (for masculine) or F (for feminine). Survival Strategy answers are in parentheses at the bottom of the exercise. Remember, they won't always agree with the grammatically correct version.

1. sedia (chair, F)

2. gabinetto (restroom, M)

3. armadio (closet, M)

4. tavola (table, F)

5. studente (male student, M)

6. passaporto (passport, M)

7. aeroporto (airport, M)

8. porta (door, F)

9. prenotazione (reservation, F)

10. corridoio (corridor, M)

11. stazione (station, F)

12. emergenza (emergency, F)

Answers: 1. la (la), 2. il (il), 3. l' (il), 4. la (la), 5. lo (il), 6. il (il), 7. l' (il), 8. la (la), 9. la (il), 10. il (il), 11. la (il), 12. l' (la)

Concrete Vocabulary

Practice identifying things around you. You can certainly get by
without this vocabulary, but it's easy to practice at home, and it is
quite possible that you might use some of these words at a hotel
or restaurant or on a train.

What is that?	Che cos'è quello?	kay <u>koh</u>-seh <u>kwayl</u>-loh?
That is ___.	(Quello) È ___.	(<u>kwayl</u>-loh) eh ___
room	la camera	lah <u>kah</u>-may-rah
floor of room	il pavimento	eel pah-vee-<u>mayn</u>-toh
chair	la sedia	lah <u>sehd</u>-yah
table	la tavola	lah <u>tah</u>-voh-lah
pen	la penna	lah <u>payn</u>-nah
wall	il muro	eel <u>moo</u>-roh
door	la porta	lah <u>por</u>-tah
ceiling	il soffitto	eel sohf-<u>feet</u>-toh
lamp	la lampada	lah <u>lahm</u>-pah-dah
light	la luce	lah <u>loo</u>-chay
window	la finestra	lah fee-<u>neh</u>-strah
book	il libro	eel <u>lee</u>-broh
paper	la carta	lah <u>kahr</u>-tah

Culture note—Accessibility

Italian towns are ancient. Most are built of stone and sit on hills.
Streets are usually narrow, paved with uneven cobblestones and
are frequently steep and twisting. Buildings are old, crammed
together, often narrow and uneven and are usually without
elevators. In other words, Italy is not a handicapped-accessible
country.

Travelers who require accessible hotels, restaurants and museums
should plan carefully, well in advance. Some guidebook listings
indicate whether a location is handicapped accessible. A good
travel agent or special tour organizer could provide invaluable
help.

Days of the Week

Monday	lunedì	*loo-nay-<u>dee</u>*
Tuesday	martedì	*mahr-tay-<u>dee</u>*
Wednesday	mercoledì	*mayr-koh-lay-<u>dee</u>*
Thursday	giovedì	*joh-vay-<u>dee</u>*
Friday	venerdì	*vay-nayr-<u>dee</u>*
Saturday	sabato	*<u>sah</u>-bah-toh*
Sunday	domenica	*doh-<u>may</u>-nee-kah*
week	la settimana	*lah sayt-tee-<u>mah</u>-nah*
weekend	il fine settimana	*eel <u>fee</u>-nay sayt-tee-<u>mah</u>-nah*
today	oggi	*<u>ohj</u>-jee*
tonight	questa notte	*<u>kway</u>-stah <u>noht</u>-tay*
tomorrow	domani	*doh-<u>mah</u>-nee*
day after tomorrow	dopodomani	*doh-poh-doh-<u>mah</u>-nee*
yesterday	ieri	*<u>yeh</u>-ree*
was	era	*<u>eh</u>-rah*
What day is today?	Che giorno è oggi?	*kay <u>johr</u>-noh eh <u>ohj</u>-jee?*
Today is ___.	Oggi è ___.	*<u>ohj</u>-jee eh ___*
What's today's date?	Che data è oggi?	*kay <u>dah</u>-tah eh <u>ohj</u>-jee?*
When?	Quando?	*<u>kwahn</u>-doh?*
morning	la mattina	*lah maht-<u>tee</u>-nah*
afternoon	il pomeriggio	*eel poh-may-<u>reej</u>-joh*
evening	la sera	*lah <u>say</u>-rah*
night	la notte	*lah <u>noht</u>-tay*
Tuesday evening	martedì sera	*mahr-tay-<u>dee</u> <u>say</u>-rah*
Sunday morning	domenica mattina	*doh-<u>may</u>-nee-kah maht-<u>tee</u>-nah*
Friday afternoon	venerdì pomeriggio	*vay-nayr-<u>dee</u> poh-may-<u>reej</u>-joh*

Culture note—Tipping

It is polite to tip anyone who performs a service for you, including those you don't see. In a hotel, you should leave a modest tip for the chambermaid on your pillow or the night table.

Exercise 2.5

Match the day of the week with the correct activity or description. Try to figure out the unfamiliar words, knowing they have something to do with days of the week. (Or peek in the dictionary at the back of this book.)

1. mezzo (middle) della settimana   A. venerdì

2. conclude il fine settimana   B. sabato

3. giovedì, ??, sabato   C. mercoledì

4. comincia (begins) la settimana   D. domenica

5. comincia il fine settimana   E. lunedì

Answers: 1) C, 2) D, 3) A, 4) E, 5) B

Exercise 2.6

"Today is Monday." Knowing that, can you answer these questions?

1. Che giorno è oggi?

2. Che giorno è domani?

3. Che giorno è dopodomani?

4. Che giorno era ieri (was yesterday)?

5. Quando è il fine settimana?

Answers: 1) (Oggi è) lunedì. 2) (Domani è) martedì. 3) (Dopodomani è) mercoledì. 4) (Ieri era) domenica. 5) (Il fine settimana è) sabato e domenica.

Culture note—Calendar weeks

Italian calendars show the week starting on Monday, not Sunday. The entire weekend is at the end of the week. If you think about it, that makes sense, since Sunday is often considered the seventh day of the week. Still, the difference can cause confusion, so don't assume that European calendars are set up the same as American ones. Take a good look when you refer to one.

Months

January	gennaio	*jayn-nah-yoh*
February	febbraio	*fayb-brah-yoh*
March	marzo	*mahr-tsoh*
April	aprile	*ah-pree-lay*
May	maggio	*mahj-joh*
June	giugno	*joon-nyoh*
July	luglio	*lool-lyoh*
August	agosto	*ah-goh-stoh*
September	settembre	*sayt-tehm-bray*
October	ottobre	*oht-toh-bray*
November	novembre	*noh-vehm-bray*
December	dicembre	*dee-chehm-bray*

Exercise 2.7
Answer the following questions with the appropriate time phrase.
Use *a* for *in.*

1. Quando è Natale (Christmas)?

2. Quando è Pasqua (Easter)?

3. Quando è la festa della mamma?

4. Quando è la festa del papà?

5. Quando è il giorno di san valentino?

6. Quando è "Thanksgiving"?

7. Quando è l'anniversario dell'indipendenza americana
   (Independence Day)?

8. Quando è la festa del lavoro (Labor Day, in U.S.)?

9. Quando è il Super Bowl?

Answers: 1) a dicembre, 2) a marzo/a aprile, 3) a maggio, 4) a giugno, 5) a
febbraio, 6) a novembre, 7) a luglio, 8) a settembre, 9) a gennaio

Culture note—Written dates

Dates in Italian are written from the smallest unit to the largest, that is, day-month-year. Christmas Day would be written as 25.12. It is especially important to remember the correct order when the date happens to be 12 or smaller. While Americans might figure out that 19.7 on a schedule indicates July 19 (as there is no 19th month), we might easily forget and read 8.7 as Aug. 7, rather than July 8.

Grammar—Definite/indefinite articles, singular

Masculine before a. . .	Def. article (the)	Indef. article (a/an)
consonant	**il** letto (the bed)	**un** letto (a bed)
vowel	**l'**albergo (the hotel)	**un** albergo (a hotel)
z or s+Consonant	**lo** stadio (the stadium)	**uno** stadio (a stadium)

Feminine before a. . .	Def. article (the)	Indef. article (a/an)
consonant	**la** camera (the room)	**una** camera (a room)
vowel	**l'**amica (the friend)	**un'**amica (a friend)

You read in the last grammar lesson what a *definite article* is: some form of *the*, used to refer to a specific (or *definite*) noun, for example, *la* lampada (*the* lamp). A different kind of article is the *indefinite article*, some form of *a* or *an*. We use an indefinite article when we aren't referring to a specific noun, but any noun of a certain type, for example, *a* lamp, instead of *the* lamp. Consider the difference in the following suggestions:

"Let's go to a movie tonight."

"Let's go to the movie tonight."

Do you see the difference? The first sentence suggests seeing *a* movie (any would do), while the second sentence suggests seeing a particular movie, *the* movie.

Like English, Italian uses different words for *a* and *the*. As we already know, *the* is either *il*, *l'* or *lo* for masculine nouns, and either *la* or *l'* for feminine nouns, depending on what letter the noun starts with. The options for *a* are a little more limited. For masculine nouns, the indefinite article (*a*) is almost always *un*. If the masculine noun starts with a *z* or with an *s plus a consonant*, then *a* is expressed as *uno*. For feminine nouns, use *una* in front of a consonant and the contracted *un'* in front of a vowel.

💣 **Survival Strategy:** If you want to simplify Italian indefinite articles, you can just use *un* for masculine nouns and *una* for feminine ones. Or, even simpler, use *un* for most words and *una* for words that end in *-a* (or that you know are feminine, like *madre*). You will be right most of the time and understood virtually all of the time.

💣 **Simplified articles**

Kind of noun	Good-guess def. article (the)	Good-guess indef. article (a/an)
Nouns ending in **-a**	**la** lampada (the lamp)	**una** lampada (a lamp)
Obviously feminine words	**la** madre (the mother)	**una** madre (a mother)
Most other nouns	**il** letto (the bed)	**un** letto (a bed)

Reality check: Remember, using simplified rules will lead to some ungrammatical choices. Still, no one will throw you out of the country if you mess up your articles. If you like to be as accurate as possible, by all means work on using definite and indefinite articles appropriately. But if you can't keep them straight, or if you are really short on time, don't worry about them.

Exercise 2.8
Concrete vocabulary review
Test yourself. Practice asking and answering questions using the concrete vocabulary from earlier in this lesson (p. 43). Try to decide whether you would use *the* or *a* if you were speaking English, and then use the Italian version of that.

| What's that? | Che cos'è quello? | *kay koh-seh kwayl-loh?* |
| That's ___. | (Quello) È ___. | *(kwayl-loh) eh ___* |

For example, you might look at a chair and ask yourself, "Che cos'è quello?" and then answer, "È una sedia." Or point at the floor: "Che cos'è quello?" Answer: "È il pavimento."

Exercise: 2.9
Can you say the following in Italian?

1. the room
2. a table
3. a pen
4. a book
5. the window
6. the book
7. the door
8. a lamp
9. a chair
10. the floor

Answers: 1) la camera, 2) una tavola, 3) una penna, 4) un libro, 5) la finestra, 6) il libro, 7) la porta, 8) una lampada, 9) una sedia, 10) il pavimento (Survival Strategy answers are the same in these cases.)

Culture note—Lodging

A hotel (*un albergo*) can span a wide range of luxury in Italy, from very basic one-star accommodations to ultra-luxurious five-star ones. For most visitors, a two- or three-star hotel is perfectly adequate. First-class hotels are often overpriced. Guesthouses (*pensioni*) use the same five-star rating system, but tend to be more casual.

Lodging

If you are arranging your own lodging, you should be familiar with the vocabulary in this section. Even if your lodging will be arranged for you, you will find some of these words and phrases useful.

Where?	Dove?	*doh-vay*
Where is ___?	Dov'è ___?	*doh-veh ___ ?*
a hotel	un albergo	*oon ahl-behr-goh*
a guesthouse	una pensione	*oon-ah payn-syoh-nay*
here	qui	*kwee*
there	là	*lah*
on the right	a destra	*ah deh-strah*
on the left	a sinistra	*ah see-nee-strah*
straight ahead	dritto	*dreet-toh*
"always straight" =keep going straight	sempre dritto	*sehm-pray dreet-toh*
Go___.	Vada ___.	*vah-dah ___*
Take ___.	Prenda ___.	*prehn-dah ___*
then	poi	*poy*

Travel tip: If you will be staying in Italy during the high season or a holiday, you should reserve your lodging as early as possible, especially in tourist centers. Even if you need lodging at a non-peak period, you can rest easy by reserving a room in advance. You can also find special deals on hotel Web sites that you may not learn about if you book a room on the spot in Italy.

In addition to the old standbys of letters and international phone calls, you can frequently make reservations via fax or e-mail. Details about accommodations and contact information can be found in travel guide books or by searching on the Web. Or you could, of course, turn to a travel agent for help.

Can you___?	Può ___?	pwoh___?
to recommend	consigliare	kohn-seel-lyah-ray
Can you recommend __?	Può consigliare ___?	pwoh kohn-seel-lyah-ray ___?
reservation	la prenotazione	lah pray-noh-tah-tsyoh-nay
I have ___.	Ho ___.	oh ___
I have a reservation.	Ho una prenotazione.	oh oon-ah pray-noh-tah-tsyoh-nay
My name is ___.	Il nome è ___.	eel noh-may eh ___
a room	una camera	oon-ah kah-may-rah
available rooms	camere libere	kah-may-ray lee-bay-ray
Do you have ___?	Ha ___?	ah ___?
Do you have rooms available?	Ha camere libere?	ah kah-may-ray lee-bay-ray?
full	completo	kohm-pleh-toh
We're full.	Siamo al completo.	syah-moh ahl kohm-pleh-toh

Culture note—Beds

A double room won't necessarily contain a double bed in Italy; often you will get two single beds instead. If a double bed is important to you, ask for *un letto matrimoniale* (a "marriage" bed).

I would like ___.	Vorrei ___.	vohr-reh-ee ___
	Desidero ___.	day-zee-day-roh ___
a double room	una camera doppia	oon-ah kah-may-rah dohp-pyah
a single room	una camera singola	oon-ah kah-may-rah seen-goh-lah
for ___ people	per ___ persone	payr ___ payr-soh-nay
with	con	kohn
without	senza	sehn-tsah
twin beds	due letti	doo-ay leht-tee
a double bed	un letto matrimoniale	oon leht-toh mah-tree-mohn-nyah-lay

a bath	un bagno	oon *bahn*-nyoh
a shower	una doccia	*oon*-ah *doht*-chah
air conditioning	l'aria condizionata	*lahr*-yah kohn-deet-tsyoh-*nah*-tah
heating	il riscaldamento	eel rees-kahl-dah-*mayn*-toh
for one night	per una notte	payr *oon*-ah *noht*-tay
for ___ nights	per ___ notti	payr ___ *noht*-tee

I'd like a double room with bath for three nights.
Vorrei una camera doppia con bagno per tre notti.
vohr-reh-ee oon-ah kah-may-rah dohp-pyah kohn bahn-nyoh payr tray noht-tee

---

Culture note—Guest registration

Overnight guests in Italy are often required to show a photo ID when they register at their hotel. As an international visitor, you may have to give the hotel staff your passport when you check in. Doing so is absolutely routine and nothing to fret about. So ignore that nagging fear that your identification will somehow end up on the black market. You will soon get your passport back and all will be fine.

---

from. . . until	da. . . a	dah. . . ah
from Saturday	da sabato	dah *sah*-bah-toh
until Tuesday	a martedì	ah mahr-tay-*dee*
How much?	Quanto?	*kwahn*-toh?
to cost	costare	koh-*stah*-ray
How much does it cost?	Quanto costa?	*kwahn*-toh *koh*-stah?
How much does ___ cost?	Quanto costa ___?	*kwahn*-toh *koh*-stah ___?
Please write it down.	Lo scriva, per favore.	loh *skree*-vah, payr fah-*vohr*-ay
Is ___ included?	Include ___?	een-*kloo*-day ___?
breakfast	la colazione	lah koh-laht-*tsyoh*-nay
sales tax	L'IVA	*lee*-vah

Culture note—Amenities

Your hotel or pension may provide different amenities than you would expect in an American hotel. If your hotel is very small or budget-minded, you may need to use a bathroom and shower down the hall, which you share with other guests. While you should receive towels to use (unless the room is very low budget), you may not get a wash cloth. Your hotel will probably provide soap, shampoo and a hair dryer, but ask first if those are important and you are staying in budget accommodations. Your bathroom might include a bidet, for private washings, either as a separate fixture or as part of the toilet. Be cautious about pulling mysterious handles or you could get a surprise.

Many old buildings (and that's most of them) won't have an elevator, or the elevator may be out of order, and hotel reception desks are frequently located on the second or third floor. Your room may be even higher. Be prepared to climb. (Yet another reason to pack light!)

Not all lodging will include heat in the winter or air conditioning in the summer. Ask, if this is important to you. ("Ha l'aria condizionata?" "Ha il riscaldamento?") Don't ask for air conditioning in winter months, even if it seems warm to you. The AC is nonfunctional when the heat is available, and Italians will view this as a crazy request.

The hotel fee may or may not include breakfast. Ask, if this is not clear. You can usually pay extra to eat breakfast in the hotel, if you would like to do so and it is not included in the room cost.

English	Italian	Pronunciation
May I ___?	Posso ___?	*pohs*-soh ___?
to see	vedere	vay-*day*-ray
May I see the room?	Posso vedere la camera?	*pohs*-soh vay-*day*-ray lah *kah*-may-rah?
to take	prendere	*prehn*-day-ray
I'll take it.	La prendo.	lah *prehn*-doh

I won't take it, thanks.	Non la prendo, grazie.	nohn lah _prehn_-doh, _graht_-tsyay

Grammar note: _It_ is expressed above as _la_ (la prendo) because it refers to _la camera_ (feminine). When _it_ refers to a masculine noun, such as _il libro_, then it is expressed as _lo_.

too	troppo	_trohp_-poh
It's too ___.	È troppo ___.	ay _trohp_-poh ___
expensive	cara*	_kah_-rah
small	piccola*	_peek_-koh-lah
noisy	rumorosa*	roo-moh-_roh_-sah
dirty	sporca*	_spohr_-kah

Grammar note: *The adjectives listed above have all been inflected to go with the word _room_ in Italian. For example, _expensive_ is expressed above as _cara_ (ending in -_a_) because it refers to _la camera_ (feminine). If we were talking about an expensive book (_il libro_—masculine), it would be _caro_, ending in -_o_.

Do you have something ___?	Ha qualcosa di ___?	ah kwahl-_koh_-sah dee ___?
cheaper	più economico	_pyoo_ ay-koh-_noh_-mee-koh
bigger	più grande	_pyoo_ _grahn_-day
quieter	più tranquillo	_pyoo_ trahn-_kweel_-loh
better	meglio	_mehl_-lyoh
receipt	la ricevuta	lah ree-chay-_voo_-tah
key	la chiave	lah _kyah_-vay

Culture note—Street noise

Italian cities are noisy. If quiet is important to you, ask for a room away from the street (_una camera che non dà sulla strada_). If you don't mind a little noise, you can sit at your window and watch Italian life bustle, roar and clatter by.

Exercise 2.10

Translate into Italian.

1. Where is the *Hotel San Carlo*, please?

2. Excuse me. Can you recommend a guesthouse?

3. Do you have rooms available?

4. I would like a double room with a bath for one night.

5. I would like a single room with a shower for three nights, from Sunday to Wednesday.

6. How much does it cost?

7. How much does a double room cost?

8. Is breakfast included?

9. How much does that cost without breakfast?

10. I'll take it.

11. That is too expensive.

12. Do you have something cheaper?

13. I would like a receipt, please.

14. Where is the key?

Answers: 1) Dov'è L'Hotel/L'Albergo San Carlo, per favore? 2) (Mi) Scusi! Può consigliare una pensione? 3) Ha camere libere? 4) Vorrei/Desidero una camera doppia con bagno per una notte. 5) Vorrei/Desidero una camera singola con doccia per tre notti, da domenica a mercoledì. 6) Quanto costa? 7) Quanto costa una camera doppia? 8) Include la colazione? 9) Quanto costa senza la colazione? 10) Lo/La prendo. 11) È troppo caro/a. 12) Ha qualcosa di più economico? 13) Vorrei/Desidero una ricevuta, per piacere. 14) Dov'è la chiave?

Culture note—Keys

Your hotel door will probably not lock automatically behind you. You will need to lock the door with the key. (And the door may be massive with the lock at eye level!) Also, in many places, you must plug the key or some other device into a slot in order to have power in your room. If you can't turn on the lights, look for someplace by the door to plug your key in.

Important words

where?	dove?	*doh-vay?*
here	qui	*kwee*
there	là	*lah*
what?	(che) cosa?	*(kay) koh-sah?*
that	quello/-a	*kwayl-loh/-lah*
who?	chi?	*kee?*
when?	quando?	*kwahn-doh?*
how long?	quanto?	*kwahn-toh?*
why?	perchè?	*payr-kay?*
how?	come?	*koh-may?*
how much?	quanto?	*kwahn-toh?*
how many?	quanti/e?	*kwahn-tee/tay?*

Culture note—Floor numbers

A cause of much confusion: The system for numbering floors differs in Europe and the United States. A European first floor is an American second floor, etc. Here's a short table to help.

United States	Italy
first floor	il piano terreno (ground floor)
second floor	il primo piano (first floor)
third floor	il secondo piano (second floor)
fourth floor	il terzo piano (third floor)

Just remember to add *one* to whatever Italian floor number you are told to go to, and you will get to the right floor.

Culture note—Energy conservation

Italian energy costs are astronomical by U.S. standards. Consequently, Italians are much more energy conscious than most Americans. One way they conserve energy is to use timed lights at night in stairwells and hallways. Look for a glowing orange button on the wall and push it for light. It will turn off automatically. In general, try to conserve resources in Italy. Your hosts will appreciate your efforts, and you will have the satisfaction of knowing that you are not one of those "wasteful Americans."

3   Restaurants and Food

Numbers (11-20)

Time to tackle more numbers. First, review the numbers zero through ten (p. 37).

Now take a look at eleven through twenty. (Practice saying the numbers out loud.)

11	undici	*oon-dee-chee*
12	dodici	*doh-dee-chee*
13	tredici	*tray-dee-chee*
14	quattordici	*kwaht-tohr-dee-chee*
15	quindici	*kween-dee-chee*
16	sedici	*say-dee-chee*
17	diciassette	*dee-chah-seht-tay*
18	diciotto	*dee-choht-toh*
19	diciannove	*dee-chahn-noh-vay*
20	venti	*vayn-tee*

Culture note—Lucky thirteen

The number 13 indicates good luck in Italy, even Friday the 13th. The only time Italians try to avoid 13 is when seating people at a table—13 is not good there. The Italian "unlucky" number is 17.

Exercise 3.1
Translate the following numbers into Italian. Try not to look at the list above.

1. eleven

2. sixteen

3. twelve

4. seventeen

5. thirteen

6. eighteen

7. fourteen

8. nineteen

9. fifteen

10. twenty

Answers: 1) undici, 2) sedici, 3) dodici, 4) diciassette, 5) tredici, 6) diciotto, 7) quattordici, 8) diciannove, 9) quindici, 10) venti

Exercise 3.2
Try some more math.

1. dodici più cinque =

2. diciotto più due =

3. sette più sei =

4. diciannove meno tre =

5. dieci più uno =

6. undici più otto =

7. diciassette meno due =

8. sedici meno quattro =

9. nove più nove =

10. otto più sei =

Answers: 1) diciassette, 2) venti, 3) tredici, 4) sedici, 5) undici, 6) diciannove, 7) quindici, 8) dodici, 9) diciotto, 10) quattordici

---

Culture note—Italian eaters

The image of the plump Italian eating piles of pasta is mostly myth. Italians are generally quite slender and don't eat much. They have only a light breakfast—if any—and a light lunch or supper. While one meal is usually more substantial, portions tend to be modest and the eating is drawn out with much conversation.

Culture note—Il bar

Il bar (the café) is central to the daily life of Italians. That's where they drink coffee and eat pastries, sandwiches and ice cream. Locals gather not only to eat and drink, but to visit, play cards and argue with each other.

Food

Food is an integral part of any culture, with so many variations that we could easily have a series of books just on Italian cuisine. Here is a summary of the most common or important food words, to give you a taste of what to expect.

Reality check: Because there are so many food words, it's hard to learn them all. Don't worry about memorizing lists of food, if you are short on time. There's not really any need to. You can look up enough in the back of this book to find out whether you are about to order ostrich or oysters. It makes sense to learn a few basic words for drinks you like and for basic foods you know you like (beef, chicken, potatoes), but don't waste precious study time on vocabulary that you will have time to look up when you need it. You will be better off concentrating on main phrases and cultural information, so you will feel comfortable entering a restaurant, ordering, eating and paying.

Where is ___?	Dov'è ___?	doh-_veh_ ___?
to recommend	consigliare	kohn-seel-_lyah_-ray
Can you ___?	Può ___?	pwoh ___?
Can you recommend ___?	Può consigliare ___?	pwoh kohn-seel-_lyah_-ray ___?
a good restaurant	un buon ristorante	oon bwohn ree-stoh-_rahn_-tay
with traditional food	con cucina tradizionale	kohn koo-_chee_-nah trah-deet-tsyoh-_nah_-lay

---

Culture note—Regional foods

Each region—and subregion—of Italy has its own food specialties. In general, foods in northern Italy are rich, based on cream, meat, butter, rice and polenta (like corn mush). Foods in the south are based on pasta, tomatoes, stronger spices, garlic and olive oil. You will usually find non-regional foods on the menu of a restaurant, but the cook really shines on the regional specialties.

Places to Eat

The following list of terms will help you decide where you want
to eat. Be aware that restaurant labels are somewhat fluid—for
example, a fancy restaurant may use a humble name. Make a habit
of checking out the posted menu (usually right outside the entrance) when choosing a place to eat.

il ristorante	restaurant, often fancy, usually a la carte, often emphasizes quality over quantity, often more expensive
la trattoria	mid-priced restaurant, cosy, simple food, local dishes, often family-run
la taverna/l'osteria	more modest than a trattoria
il bar	café, for coffee, drinks, snacks and sandwiches
il caffè	coffee shop, with alcoholic drinks. Usually doesn't have food, but possibly breakfast or sandwiches
la paninoteca	sandwich shop
la gelateria	ice cream parlor
la tavola calda	self-service buffet
la pizzeria	pizza parlor

Culture note—To sit or not to sit

In a *bar*, *caffè*, *gelateria*—anyplace that has a standing bar *and*
tables with chairs—you must decide whether you want to
stand at the bar or pay considerably more to sit down. Price
should not be your only consideration. If time is of the
essence, do as the Italians usually do, toss back your espresso
at the bar and rush back out.

If you are taking a break, though, it's well worth the cost to
sit down and relax, especially at an outdoor café. As travel
writer Rick Steves advises, don't think of it as paying an
exorbitant price to eat or drink. Think of it as renting a prime
piece of real estate. You may sit as long as you like, watching
Italian life go by.

Culture note—The traditional Italian meal

The traditional, full-blown Italian meal can regularly last more than two hours, even up to five hours on holidays. Mealtime is for so much more than food, however. Time spent with others at the table is believed to strengthen family bonds, friendship and community.

Culture note—Greetings in restaurants

It is polite to greet the people in a restaurant with a general *buon giorno* or *buona sera* when you enter. When you leave, a general *arrivederci* or *ciao* (depending on where you are) is appreciated. If you fail to acknowledge the room upon arrival and departure, you may be considered cold, reserved, or impolite.

Culture note—Giorno di riposo

Most restaurants and bars will close for one day a week, called *il giorno di riposo* (day of rest). The most common day for a *giorno di riposo* is Sunday or Monday, although it can be any day of the week. You check a place's posted hours to see when it has its day off. Museums usually have a *giorno di riposo*, as well, usually Monday, but sometimes Tuesday.

Culture note—Entering and ordering

In some sit-down eating establishments, you seat yourself, and in others you wait to be seated. (Wait a bit, if it's not clear.) If you seat yourself, don't take a table for four if there are only two of you—take a table for two. If you enter a place that has a bar, you may stand at the bar or sit at a table. If you order food or drink from a bar, you generally pay the cashier in advance for what you want, get a little receipt (*uno scontrino*), then give the receipt to whomever takes your order behind the bar. The waiter there will probably rip your receipt and give it back to you. Keep the receipt wherever you eat. You are legally required to have it when you leave.

Meals

la colazione   Breakfast is usually served from 7 to 10. A
                   hotel breakfast is usually coffee or tea, bread or
                   rolls, butter, jam, and possibly cake. Italians
                   usually have cappuccino or espresso and
                   sometimes a croissant or pastry.

il pranzo   Lunch is generally available from around 12:30
                   to 2. This is traditionally the largest meal of the
                   day and could consist of the following typical
                   courses (which would be served separately):

                   antipasto (appetizer)—cold meats or marinated
                   vegetables

                   il primo (first course)—pasta, rice or soup

                   il secondo (second course)—meat or fish,
                   sometimes with vegetable

                   il contorno (side dish)—vegetable, usually its
                   own course

                   l'insalata (salad)

                   il formaggio (cheese)

                   dolce o frutta (dessert or fruit)

                   caffè (coffee)—espresso (not cappuccino) *or*

                   digestivo (after-dinner liqueur) *or amaro* (a bitter)

                   The main meal is commonly shortened to
                   antipasto, primo, secondo with vegetable or salad,
                   and *espresso.*

la cena   Supper is generally available from around 7 to
                   around 10. It is traditionally a lighter meal,
                   often a snack or *panino* (sandwich). However, if
                   lunch was light, then supper would be larger,
                   with the same courses as the traditional lunch.

Ordering

Do you have ___?	Ha ___?	*ah ___?*
a table for ___	un tavolo per ___	*oon tah-voh-loh payr ___*
a no smoking section	una zona per non fumatori	*oon-ah dsoh-nah payr nohn foo-mah-tohr-ee*
waiter	il cameriere	*eel kah-may-ryeh-ray*
waitress	la cameriera	*lah kah-may-ryeh-rah*
to get waiter's attention	Scusi! Signore!	*skoo-zee! seen-nyoh-ray!*
to get waitress' attention	Scusi! Signora!	*skoo-zee! seen-nyoh-rah*
Ready?	È pronto/a?	*eh prohn-toh/-tah?*
What would you like?	Cosa prende? Cosa desidera?	*koh-sah prehn-day? koh-sah day-zee-day-rah?*
to recommend	consigliare	*kohn-seel-lyah-ray*
Can you ___?	Può ___?	*pwoh ___?*
something	qualcosa	*kwahl-koh-sah*
Can you recommend something?	Può consigliare qualcosa?	*pwoh kohn-seel-lyah-ray kwahl-koh-sah?*
to order	ordinare	*ohr-dee-nah-ray*
I would like ___.	Vorrei ___. Desidero ___.	*vohr-reh-ee ___ day-zee-day-roh ___*

Culture note—The waiter

Waiting on and serving people in restaurants is a respected profession in Italy. Don't hesitate to ask your waiter for recommendations. To get a waiter's attention, call "Cameriere!" If that is too much of a mouthful, use "Scusi!" or "Signore!" or both together. A raised hand or a small wave can help if you're having trouble getting someone's attention.

Culture note—The tourist menu

Many tourist-oriented eateries have a special tourist menu (*il menù turistico*) at a fixed price (*a prezzo fisso*). The set menu typically includes a first course, a second course, bread, water and wine. The meal is usually a good deal, but you don't get a lot of selection, and it's probably not the finest restaurant in town. For a harried tourist overwhelmed by unfamiliar choices, however, the limited meal suggestions can be a godsend.

I would like to order.	Vorrei ordinare.	*vohr-reh-ee ohr-dee-nah-ray*
We would like ___.	Vorremmo ___.	*vohr-rehm-moh ___*
We would like to order.	Vorremmo ordinare.	*vohr-rehm-moh ohr-dee-nah-ray*
Enjoy your meal!	Buon appetito!	*bwohn ahp-pay-tee-toh*
I like it/(___).	Mi piace (___).	*mee pyah-chay (___)*
I don't like it/ (___).	Non mi piace (___).	*nohn mee pyah-chay (___)*

Grammar note: To express that you like something in Italian, you actually say that it *is pleasing to you*. This turns things around a bit from what we're used to. Try not to think, *I like pizza*, but, rather, *Pizza is pleasing to me*. ("Mi piace la pizza.") This subtle difference doesn't matter much until you get to a plural noun. In English, it's easy to express a liking for something plural: *I like strawberries*. Same verb form as liking something singular. But in Italian, the strawberries *are pleasing to you*, and because they are plural, the verb needs to be plural, too: *Mi piacciono le fragole*.

I like them/(___).	Mi piacciono (___).	*mee pyaht-choh-noh (___)*
I don't like them/ (___).	Non mi piacciono (___).	*nohn mee pyaht-choh-noh (___)*

Culture note—Bread charge

If a basket of bread appears at your table without anyone ordering it, then bread is included in the meal price. You pay the same whether you eat no bread or several baskets of it.

Culture note—What's included?

Look over the menu (preferably the one posted outside the restaurant before you decide where to eat) to determine what is included in the posted prices. Here are terms to look for:

vino incluso—includes wine

pane e coperto inclusi—bread and cover charge included

servizio incluso or *mancia inclusa*—includes a service charge/tip. Often the amount of the service charge will be identified, generally 10%-15%.

supplemento—supplementary (extra) fee

The phrase for "not included" is *non incluso*. If you are not sure whether something is covered, ask. "È incluso _____?"

Even if service is included, it's good manners to leave a small tip, some coins up to 5% of the bill. You won't offend anyone if you overlook this, however.

Culture note—*Buon appetito!*

Before you start eating a meal, it is polite to wish your fellow diners *Buon appetito!* The closest equivalent that we have in English is "Enjoy your meal."

Similarly, before drinking with others, it is polite to hold your glass up and say *Saluti!* (Cheers!) to your companions. You may or may not clink glasses.

The Menu

menu	il menù	*eel may-<u>noo</u>*
appetizers	antipasti	*ahn-tee-<u>pah</u>-stee*
soups	zuppe	*<u>tsoo</u>-pay*
broths	brodi	*<u>broh</u>-dee*
pasta	pasta	*<u>pah</u>-stah*
meat dishes	piatti di carne	*<u>pyah</u>-tee dee <u>kahr</u>-nay*
fish	pesce	*<u>paysh</u>-shay*
seafood	frutti di mare	*<u>froot</u>-tee dee <u>mah</u>-ray*
vegetables	verdure	*vayr-<u>doo</u>-ray*
salads	insalate	*een-sah-<u>lah</u>-tah*
cheeses	formaggi	*fohr-<u>mahd</u>-joh*
fruit	frutta	*<u>froot</u>-tah*
desserts	dolci	*<u>dohl</u>-chee*

Culture note—Prego

Prego is Italian for "you're welcome," but is frequently used in situations where someone is ready for you to do something. When the waitress or person taking orders at the bar says "Prego," they are ready for you to order. Someone holding the door open for another might say "Prego" to indicate the other person should pass through. "Prego?" can also be used for "Pardon?" or "Sorry?", requesting a repetition or clarification.

Culture note—Musicians

You will see many musicians in restaurants, playing accordian or guitar and often singing, too. Some will expect to be tipped for mediocre music you did not request and will stand by your table to shame you into giving them some money. You may decide that a small tip is worth it to get rid of them, but you do not have to tip if you don't want to. The exception, of course, is if you have *asked* the musician to play something; then you do need to tip.

Drinks

drinks	bevande	bay-_vahn_-day
water	acqua	_ahk_-kwah
mineral water	acqua minerale	_ahk_-kwah mee-nay-_rah_-lay
carbonated	gassata	gahs-_sah_-tah
	frizzante	freed-_zahn_-tay
non-carbonated	naturale	nah-too-_rah_-lay
drinkable water	potabile	poh-_tah_-bee-lay
non-drinkable (warning)	non potabile	nohn poh-_tah_-bee-lay
beer	birra	_beer_-rah
wine	vino	_vee_-noh
red wine	vino rosso	_vee_-noh _rohs_-soh
white wine	vino bianco	_vee_-noh _byahn_-koh
house wine	vino della casa	_vee_-noh _dayl_-lah _kah_-sah
the wine list	la lista dei vini	lah _lee_-stah _day_-ee _vee_-nee
a glass of ____	un bicchiere di ____	oon beek-_kyeh_-ray dee ____
a carafe of ____	una caraffa di ____	_oon_-ah kah-_rahf_-fah dee ____
a bottle of ____	una bottiglia di ____	_oon_-ah boht-_teel_-lyah dee ____
tea	tè	tay
soft drink	bibita frizzante	_bee_-bee-tah freed-_zahn_-tay
juice	succo	_sook_-koh
fruit juice	succo di frutta	_sook_-koh dee _froo_-tah
milk	latte	_laht_-tay
coffee	caffè	kahf-_feh_
espresso	espresso	ays-_prehs_-soh
cappuccino	cappuccino	kahp-poot-_chee_-noh
hot chocolate	cioccolata calda	choh-koh-_lah_-tah _kahl_-dah
ice	ghiaccio	_gyaht_-choh

Culture note—Wine

Wine is the national drink of Italy, with each region producing its own specialties. Italians often drink wine, but in moderation. They usually drink it only at mealtime, one or two glasses, sipping it. It is considered very bad form to drink too much wine, and you rarely see drunk Italians. Wine is considered a healthy part of a meal and may be served before, during or after lunch and supper. You can usually order wine by the glass, carafe or bottle. If you have the assistance of a wine steward, it is polite to tip him 10% of the wine cost.

Culture note—Beverages customs

Italians generally drink mineral water at meals, either in place of or along with wine. Italian restaurants do not automatically place water on the table for customers to drink, and certainly not tap water. In fact, Italians rarely drink tap water, although it's quite safe in the northern part of the country. (You may want to stick with bottled water in the South and Sicily.) To go with local custom, you should order mineral water to drink (*acqua minerale*), and the waiter will ask whether you want *gassata/frizzante* (carbonated) or *naturale* (non-carbonated). As with other cool drinks, water will not be served with ice. You might receive ice upon request during the summer, but you are fighting a losing battle. Consider giving in and drinking cool rather than ice-cold beverages.

During meals, Italians drink wine, beer, mineral water or juice. In general, adults do not drink milk, and your waiter may be perplexed if you ask for a glass of it. While Coke is sometimes drunk during meals, many Italians are annoyed when people drink it while eating, believing that it "insults" the food, interfering with the food's flavors. You are better off ordering mineral water. If you do order a soft drink, you will notice that the servings are small by American standards, and there won't be any free refills (for coffee, either, by the way). Other than breakfast, coffee is never drunk during meals. Meals are frequently capped off with espresso, however.

Breakfast

egg	uovo	*woh-voh*
bread	pane	*pah-nay*
roll	panino	*pah-nee-noh*
croissant	cornetto	*kohr-nayt-toh*
toast	pane tostato	*pah-nay toh-stah-toh*
butter	burro	*boor-roh*
jam	marmellata	*mahr-mayl-lah-tah*
fruit juice	succo di frutta	*sook-koh dee froot-tah*
sugar	zucchero	*tsoo-kay-roh*
cream	crema	*kreh-mah*

Culture note—Breakfast drinks

Espresso or cappuccino are the most popular breakfast beverages. You may be able to get orange juice on request, but it will likely be some sort of pulpless orange drink or freshly squeezed juice. Hot chocolate is available, but it's often thick and extremely sweet, nothing like the American version.

If you are staying in a hotel, you may not be able to get coffee anywhere before 7 a.m. (a concern if you are a caffeine addict and your tour bus *leaves* at 7). You can buy something called "Caldo Caldo" in a grocery store. It's a shot of espresso packaged with some chemicals to heat it up when you want it. You press the bottom and shake the can for a while to heat it. (Follow the instructions on the container.)

Culture note—Coffees

The main coffees you will choose from in Italy are espresso, cappuccino and caffè latte. Standard *caffè* is the same as espresso.

Espresso is strong, dark coffee served in a small cup. It is the fuel Italy runs on. A typical Italian drinks at least four espressos a day, dashing in and out of bars to tank up on caffeine during breaks. Espresso is frequently drunk at the end of a meal.

Cappuccino is espresso that has steamed milk added to it. If Italians drink it at all, it is only for breakfast. Caffè latte has even more warm milk added to espresso. It is also traditionally limited to breakfast. You may order either of these drinks at any time of the day, but it's not Italian to do so.

What about decaf? Talk about un-Italian! You *can* request decaffeinated coffee. Try either "un decaf espresso" or order the brand name "Hag." Tea, by the way, is also available, if seldom drunk. Just ask for *tè* (*tay*).

You say you just want "normal" coffee? The closest you will get is *un caffè americano*, similar to (but stronger than) American coffee. As a tourist, if you order *un caffè* (meaning the strong stuff), your waiter might assume you want *un caffè americano*, so make sure you are clear if you really want espresso.

Soup

beef broth	brodo di manzo	*broh-doh dee mahn-dsoh*
chicken broth	brodo di pollo	*broh-doh dee pohl-loh*
vegetable soup	minestrone	*mee-nay-stroh-nay*
seafood chowder	cacciucco	*kaht-chook-koh*
tripe, vegetable, bean soup	busecca	*boo-zayk-kah*
soup of the day	zuppa del giorno	*tsoo-pah dayl johr-noh*
____ soup	zuppa di ____	*tsoo-pah dee ____*
creamed ____ soup	crema di ____	*kreh-mah dee ____*

Pasta

spaghetti	spaghetti	*spah-gayt-tee*
"quills"	penne	*payn-nay*
flat noodles	tagliatelle	*tahl-lyah-tehl-lay*
narrow flat noodles	fettuccine	*fayt-toot-chee-nay*
stuffed tubes baked with white sauce	cannelloni	*kahn-nayl-loh-nee*
lasagna	lasagne	*lah-zahn-nyay*
filled rings with sauce	tortellini	*tohr-tayl-lee-nee*

Culture note—Spaghetti

Italians are expert spaghetti twirlers and can neatly twist a mouthful of spaghetti around their fork with deceptive ease. In my experience, Italian spaghetti somehow seems slipperier than American. Once when I was trying to eat spaghetti the proper Italian way (if not with proper Italian flair), the noodles kept sliding off my fork. I was asked by a kindly local man, "Is this the first time you've had spaghetti?" What could I say but yes? Now I just cut my spaghetti for eating ease. It's not Italian, but it's less embarrassing than cascading noodles.

If you want to eat authentically, pull some noodles off the mound with your fork, place the end of your fork against your plate or in the bowl of the large spoon that may come with your order, and turn your fork until you have a neat mouthful. I wish you luck!

Sauces

sauce	salsa	*sahl-sah*
butter/parmesan	al burro	*ahl boor-roh*
tomato/meat	bolognese	*boh-lohn-nyay-say*
ham/cheese/eggs	carbonara	*kahr-bohn-nah-rah*
basil/garlic/cheese	pesto	*pay-stoh*

Meat

beef	manzo	*mahn-dzoh*
steak	bistecca	*bee-stayk-kah*
chicken	pollo	*pohl-loh*
pork	maiale	*mah-yah-lay*
bacon	pancetta	*pahn-chay-tah*
sausage	salsicce	*sahl-see-chay*
ham	prosciutto	*prohsh-shoot-toh*
veal	vitello	*vee-tehl-loh*
lamb	agnello	*ahn-nyehl-loh*
rabbit	coniglio	*koh-neel-lyoh*

Fish and Seafood

anchovies	acciughe	*aht-choo-gay*
prawns	gamberi	*gahm-bay-ree*
crabs	granchi	*grahn-kee*
octopus	polipo	*poh-lee-poh*
mix of small fried fish	fritto misto	*freet-toh mees-toh*

Culture note—Pea warning

The word for pea (*pisello*) is also slang for the male body part and is avoided by many Italians.

Vegetables and Salad

cabbage	cavolo	*kah-voh-loh*
carrots	carote	*kah-roh-tay*
green beans	fagiolini	*fahd-joh-lee-nee*
dried beans	fagioli	*fahd-joh-lee*
mushrooms	funghi	*foon-gee*
peas	piselli	*pee-zehl-lee*
spinach	spinaci	*spee-nah-chee*
lettuce	lattuga	*laht-too-gah*
bitter red lettuce	radicchio	*rah-deek-kyoh*

tomato	pomodoro	*poh-moh-doh-roh*
cucumber	cetriolo	*chay-tree-oh-loh*
asparagus	asparagi	*ahs-pah-rah-jee*
artichokes	carciofi	*kahr-choh-fee*
cauliflower	cavolfiori	*kah-vohl-fyoh-ree*

Culture note—Olives

Be careful when eating olives. First, they may be far saltier than you are used to. Also, Italian olives usually have pits in them. You can discretely spit the pit into your closed hand at your mouth and then place it at the edge of your plate.

---

olive	oliva	*oh-lee-vah*
onion	cipolla	*chee-pohl-lah*
mixed salad	insalata mista	*een-sah-lah-tah mees-tah*
mixed vegetables	verdura mista	*vayr-doo-rah mees-tah*
potato	patata	*pah-tah-tah*
French fries	patatine fritte	*pah-tah-tee-nay freet-tay*

Cheese

Is the cheese ___?	È il formaggio ___?	*eh eel fohr-mahd-joh ___?*
mild	dolce	*dohl-chay*
sharp	piccante	*peek-kahn-tay*
hard	duro	*doo-roh*
soft	molle	*mohl-lay*

Culture note—Salad dressing

Italians do not eat standard American salad dressings. Salads are often served already doused with vinegar and oil, or you can add your own from bottles at your table. If you eat from a salad bar, you may need to look around a bit to find the vinegar and oil bottles, but they will be there somewhere.

Fruit

fruit	frutta	*froot-tah*
apple	mela	*may-lah*
orange	arancia	*ah-rahn-chah*
pear	pera	*pay-rah*
banana	banana	*bah-nah-nah*
strawberries	fragole	*frah-goh-lay*
raspberries	lamponi	*lahm-pohn-nee*
cherries	ciliege	*chee-lyehd-jay*
peach	pesca	*pehs-kah*
grapes	uva	*oo-vah*
lemon	limone	*lee-moh-nay*

Seasoning

salt	sale	*sah-lay*
pepper	pepe	*pay-pay*
mustard	senape	*seh-nah-pay*
	mostarda	*mohs-tahr-dah*
ketchup	ketchup	*kay-choop*
mayonnaise	maionese	*mah-yoh-nay-say*
vinegar	aceto	*ah-chay-toh*
sugar	zucchero	*tsook-kay-roh*
honey	miele	*myeh-lay*
butter	burro	*boor-roh*
olive oil	olio d'oliva	*ohl-yoh doh-lee-vah*

Dessert

sweets	dolci	*dohl-chee*
cake	torta	*tohr-tah*
ice cream	gelato	*jay-lah-toh*
chocolate	cioccolato	*chohk-koh-lah-toh*
pudding	budino	*boo-dee-noh*

Tableware

a plate	un piatto	oon *pyaht*-toh
a glass	un bicchiere	oon beek-*kyeh*-ray
a fork	una forchetta	*oon*-ah fohr-*kayt*-tah
a knife	un coltello	oon kohl-*tehl*-loh
a spoon	un cucchiaio	oon kook-*kyah*-yoh
a napkin	un tovagliolo	oon toh-vahl-*lyoh*-loh
I need__.	Ho bisogno di ___.	oh bee-*zohn*-yoh dee ___

Culture note—Condiments

Condiments are not necessarily placed on the restaurant table automatically. You may need to call the waiter (*Scusi! Signore! Cameriere!*) and request what you want.

Culture note—American fast food

Travelers often dive into the local cuisine with the best intentions but find themselves hankering for familiar food after a few days. If you are dying for a Big Mac or something similar, you will find American fast food restaurants in Italian cities. The food may not be identical to what you are used to, but it will be close enough to stave off cravings, if necessary. And it's interesting to see what the chains do differently in their franchises abroad.

Paying

to pay	pagare	pah-*gah*-ray
I'd like to pay.	Vorrei pagare.	vohr-*reh*-ee pah-*gah*-ray
Check, please.	Il conto, per piacere.	eel *kohn*-toh, payr pyah-*chay*-ray

Culture note—One check

When getting ready to pay for your meal or drinks in Italy, expect to receive one check. It is not usual for the waiter to divide the check up for you. Rather than ask for separate checks (which your waiter may not appreciate), act like an Italian and have one person in your party pay. (You may want to designate who is the payer ahead of time.) Then you settle your individual bills later, if that is important to you. Just keep track of how much you owe.

Culture note—Table manners

Manners are important in Italy (part of the *bella figura*), including table manners. To be polite, you should put your napkin on your lap and wait until all are served before you eat. Don't slouch. And watch how you use your silverware.

Italians keep their fork in the left hand, knife in the right, throughout the meal, using the knife for cutting and for pushing food onto the fork.

If you are not holding the knife in your hand, you should place your right hand and forearm on the table next to the plate. (No switching the fork to your right hand!) In practice, Italians don't usually lay their hands on the table—any open hand is used for gesturing during conversation. Contrary to the custom in the United States, it is considered bad manners to place a hand on the lap during a meal.

It is customary to eat grapes and cherries with your fingers, but other fruits should be eaten with silverware. Cheese is picked up with the knife.

When you are finished eating, you should lay your silverware together (parallel) on your plate. If you are just pausing, lay your eating utensils so they face each other across the plate. Above all when eating, remember that meals are for happy socializing.

Exercise 3.3

How would you say the following in Italian?

1. Where is a restaurant?

2. We would like to order.

3. I would like a carafe of red wine, please.

4. Can you recommend something?

5. Do you have vegetable soup?

6. Can you recommend a wine?

7. I would like the soup of the day.

8. I need a fork, please.

9. Check, please!

Answers: 1) Dov'è un ristorante/una trattoria? 2) Vorremmo ordinare. 3) Vorrei/desidero una caraffa di vino rosso, per favore. 4) Può consigliare qualcosa? 5) Ha minestrone? 6) Può consigliare un vino? 7) Vorrei la zuppa del giorno. 8) Ho bisogno di una forchetta, per favore. 9) Il conto, per piacere!

Culture note—Pizza

Italian pizza is quite different from the standard American version. It is smaller, thinner, crisper, and not loaded down with toppings. Each person usually orders a separate pizza, although you may split one or order half of one, if you wish.

Toppings are also different and include artichokes, capers, anchovies and different cheeses. Some classic pizzas are:

pizza margherita—tomato, cheese, basil

pizza quattro stagioni—a variety of toppings, meat and vegetable

pizza napoletana—anchovies, ham, capers, tomatoes, cheese and oregano

pizza quattro formaggi—four types of cheese, including gorganzola

Exercise 3.4

Say several things that you like to eat or drink. For example, *Mi piacciono gli spaghetti alla bolognese. Mi piace la verdura mista.*

Now say what you *don't* like to eat or drink. For example, *Non mi piace il pesce. Non mi piace la birra.*

Culture note—Pausa

It's typical for Italians to rest for a couple of hours after lunch, if possible. This "down time" is called *pausa* and is Italy's version of the siesta. *Pausa* is thought to aid digestion, as well as spare people activity in the intense heat of summer afternoons.

Not all Italians can take a long mid-day break. A long *pausa* is more common in the country than in the city. Be aware, however, that most restaurants nonetheless close from 3 p.m. to 6 p.m.

Culture note—Paying, tipping and leaving

If you eat or drink at a bar, you usually pay in advance and can leave whenever you want without further obligation. If you are at a restaurant, you will receive a bill and may be expected to pay the waiter at your table or to take your bill and pay a cashier. In either case, you may choose to leave a small tip on the table. Don't over-tip, though. Remember, a service charge (*servizio*) is usually included on your bill. If a service charge is not included, you should tip 10%-15% of your bill.

If you eat out with an Italian, be aware that your host will probably want to pick up the tab. It is not customary to split the cost, unless it's a group of young people. Don't make a big fuss about this, or you could offend or embarrass your host.

Just as it's polite to greet the room at large when you enter a restaurant, it's nice to say a general goodbye, too. Remember, keep your receipt when you leave or technically you could face a fine.

Culture note—Smoking

Public smoking has undergone a seismic shift in Italy. In January 2005, a strict public smoking ban went into effect. As reported on National Public Radio, fully 80% of the population supported the ban, which is mind-boggling when you consider the former smoking scene in Italy. Let me describe the previous smoking culture, so you can better appreciate the magnitude of the reform.

Public Smoking, Before the Ban: Step off the plane after arriving in Italy and one of the first things you might have seen was a customs official smoking a cigarette. At six in the morning. Right next to a no-smoking sign. People would light up cigarettes at any time in almost any place.

Public smoking used to be widely tolerated. Cafès and restaurants would often be shrouded with smoke, even the rare no-smoking sections. Smoking was officially banned in some places, such as government offices, theaters and churches, but workers frequently flouted the ban. You would see smoking in banks, book shops and bakeries, almost everywhere.

That was before. What about now? Smoking has been severely restricted in public places, including in restaurants. Restaurants must have a separate room for smokers, with a separate ventilation system and automatically closing doors between the smoking and no-smoking sections. Because of the architectural limitations of the old buildings most restaurants reside in, that effectively bans smoking entirely from many restaurants.

If patrons smoke in a no-smoking section, the restaurant owner is required to advise the smoker to stop. If the patron persists, the proprietor must call the police or risk being fined thousands of euros. Will the ban be effective long term? I don't know, but the tide does seem to have turned against public smoking in Italy.

Finally, a word about smoking etiquette: to those of you who smoke and can find a smoking section in which to indulge, please don't light up during a meal—only at the end.

Exercise 3.5

Can you read a super-simplified menu? Choose what you might order for the following meals.

1. la colazione (breakfast)

    tè / espresso / cappuccino / cioccolata calda

    pane con burro e marmellata / cornetto / panini con miele

2. il pranzo (lunch) o la cena (supper)

    il primo: tortellini / riso / minestrone / zuppa del giorno

    il secondo: bistecca / pollo / coniglio / vitello

    il contorno: spinaci / fagiolini / cavolfiori / asparagi

    bevande: vino rosso / vino bianco / acqua minerale

    frutta: mela / pera / pesca / ciliege

3. lo spuntino (snack)

    espresso / acqua minerale / succo di frutta

    gelato / biscotti / panino / torta

4. a la pizzeria

    pizza margherita / pizza quattro formaggi / pizza ai funghi

4   Shopping

Numbers (0-100, by ten)

Time for more numbers. Review 0-10 (p. 37) and 11-20 (p. 57) before learning these.

0	zero	*dseh*-roh
10	dieci	*dyeh*-chee
20	venti	*vayn*-tee
30	trenta	*trayn*-tah
40	quaranta	kwah-*rahn*-tah
50	cinquanta	cheen-*kwahn*-tah
60	sessanta	says-*sahn*-tah
70	settanta	sayt-*tahn*-tah
80	ottanta	oht-*tahn*-tah
90	novanta	noh-*vahn*-tah
100	cento	*chehn*-toh

Exercise 4.1

Translate the following numbers into Italian. Try not to look at the list above.

1. ten
2. sixty
3. twenty
4. seventy
5. thirty

6. eighty
7. forty
8. ninety
9. fifty
10. one hundred

Answers: 1) dieci, 2) sessanta, 3) venti, 4) settanta, 5) trenta, 6) ottanta, 7) quaranta, 8) novanta, 9) cinquanta, 10) cento

Exercise 4.2

Give the correct number in Italian.

1. Five dozen

2. Millimeters in a centimeter

3. Minimum age for a septuagenarian

4. Two quarters = ___ cents

5. Number of U.S. senators

6. Four score

7. Two years after legal adulthood

8. "___ acres and a mule"

9. Ten trios

10. Start of the "gay" decade—18??

Answers: 1) sessanta, 2) dieci, 3) settanta, 4) cinquanta, 5) cento, 6) ottanta, 7) venti, 8) quaranta, 9) trenta, 10) novanta

Useful Vocabulary

big	grande	*grahn*-day
small	piccolo	*peek*-koh-loh
a lot	molto	*mohl*-toh
a little	un po' (di)	oon poh (dee)
hot	caldo	*kahl*-doh
cold	freddo	*frayd*-doh
good	buono	*bwoh*-noh
well	bene	*beh*-nay
bad	cattivo	kaht-*tee*-voh
enough	abbastanza	ahb-bahs-*tahn*-tsah
not enough	non abbastanza	nohn ahb-bahs-*tahn*-tsah
only	solo	*soh*-loh
also, too	anche	*ahn*-kay

Culture note—"Hot" and "cold"

If you want to say your surroundings are hot or cold ("It's hot/cold!"), use the verb *fare* (to make, to do): *Fa caldo/freddo*. If you want to express that you are overheated or chilled ("I'm cold!"), use the verb *avere* (to have, to get): *Ho caldo/freddo*.

Culture note—Commas and decimal points

In Italian numbers, commas and periods are used differently than in the American system. A comma is used to indicate decimals (where we would use a period), and a period is used to indicate thousands (where we would use a comma).

American	3,576.90
Italian	3.576,90

You will see the comma most frequently in prices. For example, *7,40 euro* means seven euros and 40 cents.

Shopping

Virtually all travelers do some shopping, even if just for postcards. Make your shopping easier by learning some useful question and answer forms.

As with food vocabulary, you will have time to look up the word for anything specific that you want to buy, so you shouldn't spend a lot of time memorizing lists of shopping items, unless you have the time or you know you are going to shop a lot.

Reality check: Shopping is one of those areas where you can get by pretty well with body language (pointing, nodding, head shaking). If you are short on language learning time, just skim this section on shopping. You are probably best off knowing how to ask *How much?* and then being familiar with numbers so you can recognize the answer.

how much	quanto	*kwahn-toh*
to cost	costare	*kohs-tah-ray*
How much does that cost?	Quanto costa?	*kwahn-toh kohs-tah?*
Please write it down.	Lo scriva, per favore.	*loh skree-vah, payr fah-voh-ray*
Do you have ___?	Ha ___?	*ah ___?*

Culture note—Pass the buck, hoard the change

There's a national game of "pass the buck" in Italy, the big "bucks" and the worn ones, that is. As you pay for things, try to hold on to your coins, small bills and fresh bills. Shop workers and museum workers *loathe* breaking larger bills, and some cashiers will try to refuse worn-out ones. The latter practice is illegal, if the money is legitimate, but it happens nonetheless.

Culture note—Customer service and the Big Sigh

Customer service is not a priority in Italy. While many restaurants and shops will have a terrifically friendly, helpful staff, that's not the case everywhere. All too often, the customer is not always right (ever right?), the customer is not king, the customer is merely a necessary nuisance to the personnel, often just getting in the way. For example, shop workers sometimes heave an exasperated sigh if you look through their displays, possibly even reprimanding you. The Big Sigh (often accompanied by a disbelieving eye roll or other extras) can appear even when you request a correction on a mistake they have made. Here are three typical examples of what Americans would consider poor customer service.

- My sister was examining leather wallets at a touristy shop near the Trevi fountain in Rome. She picked them up and looked them over before carefully replacing them. The shopworker, clearly irritated, huffed over to the display and re-straightened the rows of wallets, which were already in perfect order. The message? *Do not touch*, even though there was no sign indicating that.

- I once ordered two drinks to accompany a quick meal at McDonald's, a 7-Up and a Diet Coke. The worker who took my order set two glasses of regular Coke on my tray. I politely reminded her that I had ordered a 7-Up and a

continued

Diet Coke. She stopped in her tracks, heaved the Big Sigh (with eye roll and massive shrug), then stalked back all of four feet to the drink dispenser to get the correct drinks. Somehow I was at fault in this transaction (for not ordering the standard Coke, apparently).

- The day before taking a long train trip on a popular route, I made sure to buy my ticket and a seat reservation in advance at the train station. When turning from the counter, I looked over my papers. While the train ticket was correct, the seat reservation was for the same train *on the day after* I needed to travel. I immediately turned back to the worker and requested a correction. You can imagine what happened. Big Sigh. Slumping shoulders. Irritation. But he did make the correction.

The moral of these stories? Be prepared to occasionally encounter what we would consider poor, even churlish, service. If it happens to you, it's not personal. Try to take it in stride and don't get worked up about it, but do stand your ground if there's a problem—you will probably prevail.

to buy	comprare	*kohm-prah-ray*
I would like ___.	Vorrei ___.	*vohr-reh-ee ___*
this	questo	*kway-stoh*
that	quello	*kwayl-loh*
Can I ___?	Posso ___?	*pohs-soh ___?*
Could I ___?	Potrei ___?	*poh-treh-ee ___?*
to see	vedere	*vay-day-ray*
Could I see ___?	Potrei vedere ___?	*poh-treh-ee vay-day-ray ___?*
to look for	cercare	*chayr-kah-ray*
I'm looking for ___.	Cerco ___.	*chayr-koh ___*
toothpaste	dentifricio	*dayn-tee-free-choh*
the cash register	la cassa	*lah kahs-sah*
Where is ___?	Dov'è ___?	*doh-veh ___?*
Where is a bank?	Dov'è una banca?	*doh-veh oo-nah bahn-kah?*

Where are ___?	Dove sono ___?	*doh-vay soh-noh __?*
Where are the shoes?	Dove sono le scarpe?	*doh-vay soh-noh lay skahr-pay?*
to touch	toccare	*tohk-kah-ray*
Don't touch!	Non toccare!	*nohn tohk-kah-ray*
to help	aiutare	*ah-yoo-tah-ray*
Can I help you?	Posso aiutare?	*pohs-soh ah-yoo-tah-ray?*
Can you help me?	Può aiutarmi?	*pwoh ah-yoo-tahr-mee?*
I'm just looking.	Sto solo guardando.	*stoh soh-loh gwahr-dahn-doh*

Culture note—Haggling

Bargaining is common in some areas of Italian life, but is not acceptable everywhere. You can freely haggle over price at outdoor markets, with street vendors, for unmarked taxis and over lodging prices at small, uncrowded hotels, but that is about it. Only offer what you are willing to pay, and write it down if you think there might be any misunderstanding. If you agree on a price, you are honor-bound to buy the object.

---

sales	saldi	*sahl-dee*
to take	prendere	*prehn-day-ray*
I'll take it.	Lo/la prendo.	*loh/lah prehn-doh*
That's all.	È tutto.	*ay toot-toh*
How are you going to pay?	Come paga?	*koh-may pah-gah?*
I'll pay ___.	Pago ___.	*pah-goh ___*
with traveler's checks	con assegno turistico	*kohn ahs-sayn-nyoh too-ree-stee-koh*
	con "traveler's cheque"	*kohn "traveler's check"*
with credit card	con carta di credito	*kohn kahr-tah dee kray-dee-toh*
by cash	in contanti	*een kohn-tahn-tee*
Do you take ___?	Prende ___?	*prehn-day ___?*

Culture note—Mom-and-Pop shops

While chain stores certainly exist in Italy (anyone heard of Bennetton?), most Italian shops are of the mom-and-pop variety. They are smaller, more individual and more intimate than chains, but may have less selection and more restricted hours of business than Americans are used to.

It's been said that shopping in Italy is not a convenience but an art form. You must find the right shop at the right time of day on a day the store is not closed. As with so many things Italian, shopping in small stores is also a social experience for locals.

Stores

I'm looking for ___.	Cerco ___.	*chayr-koh* ___
Is there ___ in the area?	C'è ___ vicino?	*cheh* ___ *vee-chee-noh?*
a bank	una banca	*oo-nah bahn-kah*
a store	un negozio	*oon nay-goht-tsyoh*
a grocery store	una drogheria	*oo-nah droh-gay-ree-ah*
	un negozio di alimentari	*oon nay-goht-tsyoh dee ah-lee-mayn-tah-ree*
a market	un mercato	*oon mayr-kah-toh*
a supermarket	un supermercato	*oon soo-payr-mayr-kah-toh*
a pharmacy	una farmacia	*oo-nah fahr-mah-chee-ah*
a perfumery	una profumeria	*oo-nah proh-foo-may-ree-ah*
a gift shop	un negozio di regali	*oon nay-goht-tsyoh dee ray-gah-lee*
a bakery	una panetteria	*oo-nah pah-nayt-tay-ree-ah*
a pastry shop	una pasticceria	*oo-nah pah-steet-chay-ree-ah*
a newstand	un'edicola	*oon ay-dee-koh-lah*

a department store	un grande magazzino	oon *grahn*-day mah-gaht-*tsee*-noh
a bookstore	una libreria	*oo*-nah lee-bray-*ree*-ah
a tobacconist's shop	una tabaccheria	*oo*-nah tah-bahk-kay-*ree*-ah
a liquor store	un'enoteca	oon ay-noh-*teh*-kah
a camera store	un negozio di fotocine	oon nay-*goht*-tsyoh dee foh-toh-*chee*-nay

---

Culture note—Shop doors

Unlike in the U.S., most doors on shops and other buildings in Italy push *into* the building. Train yourself to wait a second before automatically pulling at a door and wrenching your shoulder. Look for the little *spingere* (push) sign and save some wear and tear on your arm.

---

entrance	l'ingresso	leen-*grehs*-soh
exit	l'uscita	loosh-*shee*-tah
push	spingere	*speen*-jay-ray
pull	tirare	tee-*rah*-ray
open	aperto	ah-*pehr*-toh
closed	chiuso	*kyoo*-soh
business hours	orario di apertura	oh-*rahr*-yoh dee ah-payr-*too*-rah

---

Culture note—Showing skin

Social norms for showing skin are definitely different in Italy than in the U.S. Women can go topless at beaches, and nudity is common in magazines, newspapers and on TV. You could round a city corner and be faced with an eight-foot-tall nude woman on a billboard. Yet I've read that it is illegal for men to go shirtless in the city, and it is uncommon for either sex to wear shorts in the city. Public clothing continues to be conservative.

Culture note—Business hours

Italian stores are open for more limited hours than most American stores. Be aware that most will be closed in the afternoon for a few hours, especially in smaller towns. Stores are frequently closed on Mondays, and *alimentari* (small grocery stores) usually close one afternoon in the middle of the week. Almost all businesses close for a week around Aug. 15 for summer vacation (*ferragosto*) and on religious holidays.

Retail and office hours are very flexible. Typically, stores and businesses will open around 9, close from around 1-4 for lunch, and open again until 7 or 8. Shops are closed Sunday, except for fresh pasta shops (which are open in the morning) and tourist shops.

Post offices, banks and government offices usually close for the day at 1:30 or 2, although banks may open again for an hour in the afternoon (e.g., 3-4). Banks are closed on weekends. Post offices are open Saturday until noon.

Outdoor food markets are only open in the morning and shut down before lunch.

More shopkeepers are staying open over lunch, then closing earlier in the evening, a schedule called *orario nonstop* or *orario continuato*. Some *tabacchi*, *farmacie* and *benzinai* (gas stations) are open 24 hours.

Exercise 4.3

Translate the following into Italian.

1. Where is a gift shop?

2. I'm looking for the cash register.

3. How much does that cost?

4. Excuse me. Where is a pharmacy, please?

5. I'm looking for a supermarket.

6. I'm just looking.

Answers: 1) Dov'è un negozio di regali? 2) Cerco la cassa. 3) Quanto costa? 4) Scusi. Dov'è una farmacia, per favore? 5) Cerco un supermercato. 6) Sto solo guardando.

Culture note—Common stores

Tabacchi (tobacco shops)
offer basic items such as tobacco, transportation tickets, newspapers, stamps, postcards and trinkets. Many also sell additional items, to the point where they look like full-fledged gift shops or bakeries or bars. The sign indicating a *tabaccheria* is a white T on a black background, or sometimes the reverse.

Farmacie (pharmacies)
offer anything related to health or hygiene—medicine, foot pads, razors, shampoo, facial tissues, sanitary napkins, thermometers, disinfectants, cough drops. Pharmacists also diagnose minor ailments and provide stronger medicines than U.S. pharmacies allow without a doctor's prescription.

Negozi di abbigliamento (clothing stores)
do not provide the hands-on experience of American shops. You are usually not allowed to browse. Rather, the salesperson asks what you want in what size. *Don't* help yourself, looking through stacks of clothing, or you will likely be reprimanded.

If you try clothes on, don't expect privacy in the dressing room. Do try clothing before buying it, though. If you change your mind after buying it, you probably won't get a refund, even if the merchandise is flawed. The best you can usually hope for is a store credit.

Supermercati (supermarkets)
offer a wide range of food and other products, although some stores will be small by American standards. Have your money at the ready to pay and be prepared to sack your own purchases. You may have to pay for plastic bags, if you need them.

Clothing

clothing	l'abbigliamento	lahb-beel-lyah-mayn-toh
blouse	la camicetta	lah kah-mee-chayt-tah
shirt	la camicia	lah kah-mee-chah
T-shirt	la T-shirt	lah tee-shirt
pants	i pantaloni	ee pahn-tah-loh-nee
jeans	i jeans	ee jeenz
skirt	la gonna	lah gohn-nah
dress	il vestito	eel vays-tee-toh
shorts	gli shorts	lyee shohts
sweater	il maglione	eel mahl-lyoh-nay
sweatshirt	la felpa	lah fayl-pah
bathing suit/trunks	il costume da bagno	eel kohs-too-may dah bahn-nyoh
hat	il cappello	eel kahp-pehl-loh
underpants	le mutande	lay moo-tahn-day
bra	il reggiseno	eel rayj-jee-say-noh
socks	i calzini	ee kahl-tsee-nee
tie	la cravatta	lah krah-vaht-tah
jacket	la giacca	lah jahk-kah
coat	il cappotto	eel kahp-poht-toh
gloves	i guanti	ee gwahn-tee
shoes	le scarpe	lay skahr-pay
sandals	i sandali	ee sahn-dah-lee
handbag	la borsetta	lah bohr-sayt-tah
umbrella	l'ombrello	lohm-brehl-loh

Colors

color	colore	koh-loh-ray
black	nero	nay-roh
white	bianco	byahn-koh
red	rosso	rohs-soh
yellow	giallo	jahl-loh
green	verde	vayr-day

blue	blu	*bloo*
brown	marrone	*mahr-roh-nay*
purple	viola	*vee-oh-lah*
gray	grigio	*gree-joh*
pink	rosa	*roh-sah*
orange	arancione	*ah-rahn-choh-nay*
beige	beige	*bayzh*
light	chiaro	*kyah-roh*
dark	scuro	*skoo-roh*

To indicate that a color is light or dark, you use the color name followed by the word *scuro* (for dark) or *chiaro* (for light).

| dark ___ | (color) scuro | ___ *skoo-roh* |
| light ___ | (color) chiaro | ___ *kyah-roh* |

For example, navy blue is *blu scuro* and light green is *verde chiaro*.

Culture note—Style

Most Italians don't look as if they have just stepped out of a fashion magazine. You don't have to either. You can have a wonderful visit in Italy even if you are on the frumpy side. (I speak from experience here.)

That said, there's no denying that style is very important in Italy. Most Italians try to look good all the time. Many qualify as "dressed up" by casual American standards, even in summer heat. Their clothing is elegant, conservative, and of high quality. They don't wear loud color combinations or jarring patterns. They prefer solids in quiet colors. In other words, no Hawaiian shirts.

Colors are particularly subdued in winter, when much of Italy dresses in basic black. You might see some gray, navy blue or brown for variety, but you really can't go wrong with black, even all black.

In general, Italians don't like a lot of ornamentation. Most don't wear much jewelry or makeup.

Culture note—Italian products

What to buy when in Italy? Italy specializes in the following products:

cameos, ceramics (especially Naples), glass (especially Venice), lace, leather (especially Tuscany), marble (especially near Genoa) and marquetry (inlaid wood).

Don't assume all these products are a good value, however. Look them over closely before buying. Not all will be genuine Italian or of high quality.

Exercise 4.4

What colors are the following items?

1. milk
2. a dollar bill
3. bricks
4. pumpkins
5. chocolate

6. strawberry ice cream
7. dandelion
8. sapphires
9. slate
10. amethests

Answers: 1) bianco, 2) verde, nero, bianco 3) rosso, 4) arancione, 5) marrone, 6) rosa, 7) giallo, 8) blu, 9) grigio o nero, 10) viola

Culture note—Shoes

The ubiquitous white tennis shoe is also seen in Italy—mostly on American tourists. Italians wear few sport shoes, and most of those aren't white.

Inside, Italians remove their outdoor shoes and wear indoor shoes or slippers. You shouldn't pad around indoors in your socks or (horrors!) barefoot (although whatever you do behind your closed hotel door is your own business). Wear your shoes if you're anywhere people can see you, including to breakfast.

Be aware that it is never acceptable to place your feet on furniture, even on a train. Doing so is gauche and does not support the *bella figura*.

Miscellaneous Purchases

I need ___.	Ho bisogno di ___.	*oh bee-sohn-nyoh dee* ___
I would like ___.	Vorrei ___.	*vohr-reh-ee* ___
a newspaper	un giornale	*oon johr-nah-lay*
an American newspaper	un giornale americano	*oon johr-nah-lay ah-may-ree-kah-noh*
a magazine	una rivista	*oo-nah ree-vees-tah*
cigarettes	sigarette	*see-gah-rayt-tay*
a candy	una caramella	*oo-nah kah-rah-mehl-lah*
a battery	una pila	*oo-nah pee-lah*
eyeglasses	occhiali	*ohk-kyah-lee*
sunglasses	occhiali da sole	*oh-kyah-lee dah soh-lay*
a camera	una macchina fotografica	*oo-nah mah-kee-nah foh-toh-grah-fee-kah*
a roll of film	un rollino	*oon rohl-lee-noh*
a ballpoint pen	una penna a sfera	*oo-nah payn-nah a sfeh-rah*
facial tissues	fazzoletti di carta	*faht-tsoh-layt-tee dee kahr-tah*
a bar of soap	una saponetta	*oo-nah sah-poh-nayt-tah*
a shampoo	uno shampoo	*oo-noh shahm-poo*
a toothpaste	un dentifricio	*oon dayn-tee-free-choh*
a deodorant	un deodorante	*oon day-oh-doh-rahn-tay*
razor blades	lamette da barba	*lah-mayt-tay dah bahr-bah*
a shaving cream	una crema da barba	*oo-nah kreh-mah dah bahr-bah*
an aftershave	un dopobarba	*oon doh-poh-bahr-bah*
a perfume	un profumo	*oon proh-foo-moh*

Exercise 4.5
Match the following items with where you could buy them.

1. libra
2. giornale
3. vino
4. rollino
5. torta
6. aspirina
7. pane

A. farmacia
B. panetteria
C. tabaccheria
D. enoteca
E. libreria
F. pasticceria
G. edicola

Answers: 1) E, 2) G, 3) D, 4) C, 5) F, 6) A, 7) B

(Note: You could actually find most of these items in more than one type of store. This exercise was overly picky!)

Exercise 4.6
Translate the following into Italian.

1. I need a battery, please.

2. Where are the shoes?

3. I'm looking for a blouse.

4. I would like facial tissues, please.

5. I need razor blades.

6. Do you have sunglasses?

7. Where is the shampoo?

8. I'm looking for a jacket.

9. I would like an American newspaper.

10. Where are the pants?

Answers: 1) Ho bisogno di una pila, per favore. 2) Dove sono le scarpe? 3) Cerco una camicetta. 4) Vorrei fazzoletti di carta, per favore. 5) Ho bisogno di lamette da barba. 6) Ha occhiali da sole? 7) Dov'è lo shampoo? 8) Cerco una giacca.. 9) Vorrei un giornale americano. 10) Dove sono i pantaloni?

Culture note—Bags

It's very common to carry a bag in Italy, even for men, but not a fanny pack. A fanny pack screams "tourist" and can even become a security risk.

Culture note—Toiletries

If you are choosy about the toiletries you use, bring plenty along with you. Italy has a wide selection of personal hygiene products, but finding a specific American brand of shampoo or deodorant can be difficult.

Culture note—Perfume

While Italians generally use makeup sparingly, they are fond of scents. You will notice a lot of perfume and aftershave. If you enjoy scents, you may want to visit *una profumeria* and try some of the many perfumes and aftershaves available.

Grammar—Adjective endings, singular

Masculine—singular	Feminine—singular
il/un vestito rosso (the/a red dress)	la/una cravatta rossa (the/a red tie)
il/un ponte vecchio (the/an old bridge)	l'/un'abitazione vecchia (the/an old house)
il/un vestito verde (the/a green dress)	la/una cravatta verde (the/a green tie)

If we want to describe objects, such as the color of things, we use adjectives. In English, adjectives are very straightforward; we can use the same adjective in the same form with all nouns for which it makes sense, for example, a *red* dress or a *red* tie.

You know that in Italian, all nouns are either masculine or feminine, and which one they are affects which form of *the* or *a/an* that we are supposed to use with them. It is probably no surprise, then, to learn that the form of an adjective is determined by a noun's gender.

The "standard" ending for most adjectives is *-o*, as in *rosso* (red). You of course remember that *-o* is also the "standard" ending for masculine nouns, as in *il vestito* (the dress). To say that the dress is red, we call it *il vestito rosso*. We do not need to change the *-o* adjective ending when it describes a masculine noun. It already "fits" there.

When an *-o* adjective is used with a feminine noun, however, it needs to take an *-a* ending. For example, while *il vestito rosso* (the red dress) is perfectly correct, because *vestito* is masculine, if we describe a feminine object, such as a tie (*la cravatta*), then the word for *red* should also be in its feminine form: *la cravatta rossa*. (These examples also remind us that objects are not "male" or "female" based on whom we would associate them with, men or women. Their "gender" is solely a matter of grammar.)

It often happens that the noun and adjective endings will match—either *-o* and *-o* or *-a* and *-a* (as discussed above)—but that's not always the case. For example, not all masculine or feminine nouns end in *-o* or *-a*. Many end in *-e*. The adjective ending is still supposed to show whether the noun is masculine or feminine though, if possible. Consider, for example,

il ponte (M)

l'abitazione (F)

Il ponte (the bridge) is masculine, so an adjective, such as *vecchio* (old), should also be in its masculine form: *il ponte vecchio*. If we wanted to talk about an old house, we would want to know that *abitazione* is feminine so we could put the right ending on that: *l'abitazione vecchia*.

Not just nouns end in *-e*, though. Many adjectives do as well, such as *verde* (green), *marrone* (brown) and *beige*. These adjectives will keep their *-e* ending regardless of whether the noun is masculine or feminine. For example,

il vestito verde (the green dress)

la cravatta verde (the green tie)

This gets a little tricky in the unusual cases when both the noun and the adjective end in *-e*, for example, *l'abitazione marrone* (the brown house) or *il ponte marrone* (the brown bridge). In these cases, the only clue we have to the noun's gender is in the article, *il/la* or *un/una*, and even that doesn't help us with a form that "hides" gender, such as *l'abitazione marrone*. Just looking at the noun, article and adjective ending of *l'abitazione marrone*, we can't tell whether it is masculine or feminine. Fortunately, such cases are in the minority. (Note: The adjective *rosa* is irregular because it ends in *-a* for masculine and feminine nouns. *Blu* also stays the same for both genders, with no change in ending.)

As you have probably noticed from the examples given here, the adjective usually comes after the noun in Italian. This takes a little practice to get used to, but is not particularly difficult.

Exercise 4.7

Are these adjectives in a form to match masculine nouns, feminine nouns, or either?

1. cortese (polite)
2. caro (expensive)
3. arancione (orange)
4. piccolo (small)
5. economica (cheap)
6. nuova (new)
7. giovane (young)
8. rosa (pink)
9. lungo (long)
10. stretta (tight)

Answers: 1) E, 2) M, 3) E, 4) M, 5) F, 6) F, 7) E, 8) E (*irregular), 9) M, 10) F

Exercise 4.8

Match up the English phrases with the correct Italian ones.

1.	the new table	A.	una camera libera
2.	an American passport	B.	un ristorante nuovo
3.	the English woman	C.	la donna inglese
4.	the old bed	D.	il letto vecchio
5.	the English newspaper	E.	la tavola nuova
6.	an available room	F.	un passaporto americano
7.	a new restaurant		
8.	the American man	G.	l'uomo americano
		H.	il giornale inglese

Answers: 1) E, 2) F, 3) C, 4) D, 5) H, 6) A, 7) B, 8) G

Exercise 4.9

How do you say the following in Italian?

1.	the white paper	5.	a dark red skirt
2.	a black hat	6.	the gray shirt
3.	the blue handbag	7.	the light green blouse
4.	the yellow umbrella	8.	the pink sweater

Answers: 1) la carta bianca, 2) un cappello nero, 3) la borsetta blu, 4) l'ombrello giallo, 5) una gonna rossa scura, 6) la camicia grigia, 7) la camicetta verde chiara, 8) il maglione rosa

---

Culture note—Quality

Americans love a bargain and frequently choose quantity over quality. Most Italians are the reverse—they prefer quality over quantity and are willing to pay for it. Don't be surprised if prices are higher for goods than you are used to in the United States, especially if the dollar is weak.

Useful Vocabulary

open	aperto	*ah-pehr-toh*
closed	chiuso	*kyoo-soh*
early	presto	*preh-stoh*
late	tardi	*tahr-dee*
more	più	*pyoo*
less	meno	*may-noh*
expensive	caro	*kah-roh*
cheap	economico	*ay-koh-noh-mee-koh*
nearby	vicino	*vee-chee-noh*
faraway	lontano	*lohn-tah-noh*
up	su	*soo*
down	giù	*joo*

Culture note—Overcharging

Keep an eye on what you are being charged when you pay for something, especially in tourist areas. Slight overcharging or not returning all of your change are common occurrences.

Culture note—Receipts

Make sure you get a receipt (*uno scontrino* or *una ricevuta*) any time you pay money for something. The shopkeeper is legally required to provide one, and you are legally required to ask for it if he doesn't. The tax police can fine you if you don't have a receipt for even the smallest purchase. Keep the receipt until you get home. Tax avoidance is a huge problem in Italy, and requiring receipts is one way to crack down on the "hidden economy." Sales tax, by the way, is always included in the price of purchases.

Remember, a standard receipt is *una ricevuta*, but if you pay before receiving something, such as when you order coffee or ice cream at a bar, the little receipt you hand to the worker to get your order (like a voucher) is *uno scontrino*.

5   Sightseeing

Numbers (21-99)

Once you learn how to count in the twenties, thirties, etc., up to 100, you will have the hardest part of the number system behind you. Review the numbers you already know before you attack the new ones: count from 0 to 20, then from 0 to 100 by tens. Then look at the new numbers below.

20	venti	*vayn*-tee
21*	ventuno	vayn-*too*-noh
22	ventidue	vayn-tee-*doo*-ay
23	ventitré	vayn-tee-*tray*
24	ventiquattro	vayn-tee-*kwaht*-troh
25	venticinque	vayn-tee-*cheen*-kway
26	ventisei	vayn-tee-*seh*-ee
27	ventisette	vayn-tee-*seht*-tay
28*	ventotto	vayn-*toht*-toh
29	ventinove	vayn-tee-*noh*-vay
30	trenta	*trayn*-tah
31*	trentuno	trayn-*too*-noh
32	trentadue	trayn-tah-*doo*-ay
43	quarantatré	kwah-rahn-tah-*tray*
54	cinquantaquattro	cheen-kwahn-tah-*kwaht*-troh
65	sessantacinque	says-sahn-tah-*cheen*-kway
76	settantasei	sayt-tahn-tah-*seh*-ee
87	ottantasette	oht-tahn-tah-*seht*-tay
98*	novantotto	noh-vahn-*toht*-toh
99	novantanove	noh-vahn-tah-*noh*-vay

* Numbers ending in -*uno* and -*otto* use contracted forms.

Using the table below as a guide, count from 21-99. Combine the numbers of the right column with the number 20 to get 21-29, then go through all combinations with the number 30, and so on, until you reach 100. Run through all the numbers a couple of times, until they start to feel a little more natural.

Forming numbers 21-99

20	(venti)	1	(uno)*
30	(trenta)	2	(due)
40	(quaranta)	3	(tré)
50	(cinquanta)	4	(quattro)
60	(sessanta)	5	(cinque)
70	(settanta)	6	(sei)
80	(ottanta)	7	(sette)
90	(novanta)	8	(otto)*
		9	(nove)

* Remember to contract when the number ends in *-uno* or *-otto*.

Exercise 5.1
Can you read the following numbers out loud?

1.	93	6.	72
2.	61	7.	56
3.	27	8.	65
4.	88	9.	34
5.	49	10.	41

Answers: 1) novantatré, 2) sessantuno, 3) ventisette, 4) ottantotto, 5) quaranta-nove, 6) settantadue, 7) cinquantasei, 8) sessantacinque, 9) trentaquattro, 10) quarantuno

---

Culture note—Public affection

Not only will you see ample public displays of platonic affection in Italy, but romantic affection as well. Romantic kissing and hugging may occur on the street, on trains, on the subway and in other places you might not expect it. Just avert your eyes if the couple sitting across from you gets too friendly for your comfort, and try to remember that Italy is a crowded country, and many young people don't have a lot of options for privacy.

Units of Time

how long?	quanto dura?	*kwahn-toh <u>doo</u>-rah?*
year	l'anno	*<u>lahn</u>-noh*
month	il mese	*eel <u>may</u>-say*
week	la settimana	*lah sayt-tee-<u>mah</u>-nah*
day	il giorno	*eel <u>johr</u>-noh*
hour	l'ora	*<u>loh</u>-rah*
minute	il minuto	*eel mee-<u>noo</u>-toh*
second	il secondo	*eel say-<u>kohn</u>-doh*

Excercise 5.2

Complete the following statements about units of time.

1. Sessanta secondi fanno (make) _____.

2. Sessanta minuti fanno _____.

3. Ventiquattro ore fanno _____.

4. Sette giorni fanno _____.

5. Quattro settimane fanno _____.

6. Dodici mesi fanno _____.

Answers: 1) un minuto, 2) un'ora, 3) un giorno, 4) una settimana, 5) un mese, 6) un anno

---

Culture note—La piazza and the evening stroll

The *piazza* is usually the heart of an Italian town, where the most important buildings are, where festivals are held, where markets are set up, where people go to see and be seen. Expect to see entire families out in the *piazza* in the evening, eating ice cream, gathering for coffee, walking hand in hand, even teaching children to ride bicycles.

This evening stroll—*la passeggiata*—is a social ritual in good weather. It spills beyond the *piazza* to the main streets in town. People dress well for *la passeggiata*, to make a good impression on others while they check each other out.

Grammar—Noun plurals

Gender	Singular	Plural
Masculine	-o/-e	-i
Feminine	-e	-i
	-a	-e

We don't get very far in a new language before we want to start talking about more than one thing at a time, using plural forms, in other words. This is a good time to discuss plural forms, because we frequently want to talk about more than one minute, hour, day, or other unit of time.

The Italian rules for making plural forms are quite regular. But while Italian plurals are good about following the rules, the rules themselves can seem complicated to those of us learning the language.

Starting with the nouns themselves, we know that the masculine forms end in *-o* or *-e* when they are singular. Their ending changes to *-i* to show plural. For example, one book is *un libro*, but two books are *due libri*. One year is *un anno*, three years are *tre anni*. One male student is *uno studente*, four male students are *quattro studenti*.

We know that feminine nouns can end in *-e*, like masculine ones, or in *-a*. The *-e* ending nouns are easy for us to make plural now, because they follow the same pattern as the *-e* ending masculine nouns: the *-e* changes to *-i*. One mother, for example, is *una madre*, but two are *due madri*. The "classic" ending for feminine nouns, though, is *-a*. The *-a* ending changes to *-e* to form plurals. For example, *una casa* (one house) becomes *tre case* (three houses), and *un'ora* (one hour) becomes *quattro ore* (four hours). This can get a little confusing, because if we see a word that ends in *-e*, we have to figure out whether it's a singular noun that ends in *-e* or the plural of a noun that ends in *-a*. Many noun plurals are included in the Italian-English dictionary at the back of this book.

Reality check: If you find plurals too confusing, just ignore them. Anyone would understand *tre giorno* just as well as you would understand *three day*. Plural forms are a nice touch of accuracy, but they add very little to communication.

Exercise 5.3
Make the plural forms for units of time.

1. anno

2. mese

3. settimana

4. giorno

5. ora

6. minuto

7. secondo

Answers: 1) anni, 2) mesi, 3) settimane, 4) giorni, 5) ore, 6) minuti, 7) secondi

Exercise 5.4
Can you answer the following questions? Remember that *quanti* (or *quante*, for feminine) means *how many*.

1. Quanti mesi ha un anno?

2. Quante settimane ha un mese?

3. Quanti giorni ha una settimana?

4. Quante ore ha un giorno?

5. Quanti minuti ha un'ora?

6. Quanti secondi ha un minuto?

Answers: 1) Un anno ha 12 (dodici) mesi. 2) Un mese ha 4 (quattro) settimane. 3) Una settimana ha 7 (sette) giorni. 4) Un giorno ha 24 (ventiquattro) ore. 5) Un'ora ha 60 (sessanta) minuti. 6) Un minuto ha 60 (sessanta) secondi.

Study tip: If you master this much of Italian plurals, you will be doing very well. You can look at the upcoming explanations to see how other parts of the language change to show plurals, but only very motivated readers will want to invest the time to become proficient at all aspects of Italian plurals.

💣* **Survival Strategy:** If even this much discussion of plurals is making your head spin, don't dispair. Really, you can get your point across quite well by using plural numbers and singular noun forms. Asking a hotel clerk for a room with *due letto* (two bed) may not be pretty, but it will work just fine.

Grammar—Definite articles (*the*), plurals

Gender	Singular	Plural
Masculine		
before a consonant	il	i
before a vowel	l'	gli
before z or s+consonant.	lo	gli
Feminine		
before a consonant	la	le
before a vowel	l'	le

We know from experience that the many forms of *the* in Italian can be confusing. Unfortunately, that complexity continues through the plural versions, although there are fewer forms to contend with. The masculine *il* changes to *i* in the plural, and *l'* and *lo* both change to *gli* (pronounced *lyee*). For example, *il letto* (the bed) becomes *i letti* (the beds). *L'anno* (the year) becomes *gli anni* (the years). And *lo studente* (the male student) becomes *gli studenti* (the male students).

The feminine forms of *the* are also simplified a bit in the plural. Both *la* and *l'* are replaced by *le*. For example, *la casa* (the house) becomes *le case* (the houses). *L'ora* (the hour) becomes *le ore* (the hours).

Culture note—Roman water

If you get thirsty tromping around Rome, you can safely drink the city water out of old public drinking fountains (not the big display fountains—the small ones that release just a stream at drinking height). Plug the big hole on the bottom of the faucet with your thumb, and drinking water will shoot out of the small hole on the top. The public water is safe to drink unless it's labeled *non potabile.*

Culture note—Pedestrian hazards

Most tourists in Italy walk a lot. You should be alert to the following potential hazards for pedestrians.

—Quiet cars can sneak up on you unawares. Look carefully before you step into a street, even if you don't hear any traffic.

—Traffic signals and turn signals are "only a suggestion." Don't rely on them. Crossing major streets can require a major leap of faith. When crossing a busy street, try to stick with a crowd of locals (like glue!) for safety's sake. They will be much better at gauging when to enter traffic and conveying their purpose to drivers.

—Watch out for motorbikes buzzing down alleys, along sidewalks and through crowded streets. They seem to come from nowhere sometimes and often cut very close to pedestrians. After a few encounters with swarms of Vespas (a popular Italian motorbike), you will agree that they are well named (*vespa* = wasp).

—Keep an eye on the ground for dog messes.

—Do not assume that early morning puddles on the sidewalk are from rain. Public toilets can be scarce, especially at those hours.

—Watch out for bicyclists. Bike paths are not common in Italy, and bicycles mix in the same jumble as cars, motorbikes and pedestrians at or on the street.

Grammar—Noun plurals (summary)

	Singular	Plural
Noun endings	-o/-e	-i
	-a	-e
Definite art. (*the*)		
Masculine	il	i
	l'/lo	gli
Feminine	l'/la	le

Exercise: 5.5

Practice making the following noun phrases plural.

1. la scarpa (shoe)
2. la gonna (skirt)
3. il gatto (cat)
4. il cane (dog)
5. la ricevuta (receipt)
6. il bicchiere (glass)
7. il giorno (day)
8. il gabinetto (bathroom)
9. lo stato (state)
10. la donna (woman)
11. il duomo (cathedral)
12. la cartolina (postcard)
13. il francobollo (stamp)
14. l'automobile (car) (F)
15. l'ingresso (entrance)

Answers: 1) le scarpe, 2) le gonne, 3) i gatti, 4) i cani, 5) le ricevute, 6) i bicchieri, 7) i giorni, 8) i gabinetti, 9) gli stati, 10) le donne, 11) i duomi, 12) le cartoline, 13) i francobolli, 14) le automobili, 15) gli ingressi

Sightseeing

Seeing the sights is a major part of most trips abroad. Learn some basic vocabulary to find your way more easily.

Where is ___?	Dov'è ___?	*doh-veh* ___ ?
tourist information office	l'ufficio turistico	*loof-fee-choh too-rees-tee-koh*
map	la mappa	*lah mahp-pah*
	la carta	*lah kahr-tah*

city	la città	*lah cheet-<u>tah</u>*
downtown area	il centro	*eel <u>chehn</u>-troh*
old part of town	la parte vecchia della città	*lah <u>pahr</u>-tay <u>vayk</u>-kyah <u>dayl</u>-lah cheet-<u>tah</u>*
historical center	il centro storico	*eel <u>chehn</u>-troh <u>stoh</u>-ree-koh*
cathedral	la cattedrale	*lah kaht-tay-<u>drah</u>-lay*
	il duomo	*eel <u>dwoh</u>-moh*
church	la chiesa	*lah <u>kyay</u>-zah*

Culture note—Church attire

The Vatican, sitting in the middle of Rome, is the center of the Catholic church, and Italy is a very Catholic country. You will see churches, cathedrals, chapels, and prayer niches on seemingly every street; crucifixes and religious statues inside and out; and priests, nuns and monks scurrying about. Aside from church officials, most Italians are not practicing Catholics these days. They still respect the church, however, and expect others to show respect as well, and that includes proper dress.

In churches you should cover your torso and upper arms, you shouldn't wear shorts or very short skirts, and men should remove any cap or hat.

---

museum	il museo	*eel moo-<u>zeh</u>-oh*
palace	il palazzo	*eel pah-<u>laht</u>-tsoh*
castle	il castello	*eel kahs-<u>tehl</u>-loh*
bridge	il ponte	*eel <u>pohn</u>-tay*
fountain	la fontana	*lah fohn-<u>tah</u>-nah*
market	il mercato	*eel mayr-<u>kah</u>-toh*
park	il parco	*eel <u>pahr</u>-koh*
garden	il giardino	*eel jahr-<u>dee</u>-noh*
square	la piazza	*lah <u>pyaht</u>-tsah*
stadium	lo stadio	*loh <u>stah</u>-dyoh*

Culture note—La guardaroba

You will be expected to check your coat and bags at many tourist sights, even if you don't want to. Look for the room or counter labeled *Guardaroba* (checkroom). If you are not charged for this service, you should give a small tip.

---

entrance	l'ingresso	*leen-grehs-soh*
exit	l'uscita	*loosh-shee-tah*
admission	l'entrata	*layn-trah-tah*
	l'ingresso	*leen-grehs-soh*
ticket	il biglietto	*eel beel-lyayt-toh*
adult	l'/l' adulto/-a	*lah-dool-toh/-tah*
child	il/la bambino/-a	*eel/lah bahm-bee-noh/-nah*
free admission	ingresso gratuito	*een-grehs-soh grah-too-ee-toh*
prohibited/no ___	vietato	*vyay-tah-toh*
no entry	ingresso vietato	*een-grehs-soh vyay-tah-toh*
no smoking	vietato fumare	*vyay-tah-toh foo-mah-ray*
no using flash photography	vietato usare il flash	*vyay-tah-toh oo-zah-ray eel "flash"*

Culture note—City bus tours

Many cities offer sightseeing overviews by bus, often allowing you to hop on and off the bus at major sights. These tours can be well worth the money for the convenient transportation they provide, particularly in unpleasant weather. If it's raining, you can stay dry inside. And even if the weather's nice, it's much easier to ride the sightseeing buses around than the city buses. Check at the tourist information office (*l'ufficio turistico*—usually at the train station) for listings.

Culture note—Cobblestone streets

Many Italian streets are paved with cobblestones, which are picturesque but can be rough on the feet. The stones can get very slick when wet. If you will be walking a lot, wear thick-soled, sturdy shoes that are well broken in. Any blisters you develop will hurt twice as badly on the uneven walking surface.

Culture note—Tipping and donations

If you have a guided tour of a sight, it is customary to slip your guide a small tip at the end of the tour. Also, while most churches are open for free viewing, they do appreciate a contribution to the donation box, usually located near the entrance. Most Italians do not donate when they view a church, however.

Exercise 5.6

Translate into Italian.

1. Where is the entrance?

2. I need a city map, please.

3. I need a ticket.

4. How much does a ticket cost?

5. Where is the cathedral?

6. I'm looking for the city center.

7. Straight ahead and then left.

8. I see the park.

9. I would like to buy two tickets.

10. Two adults.

Answers: 1) Dov'è l'ingresso? 2) Ho bisogno di una mappa/carta (della città), per favore. 3) Ho bisogno di un biglietto. 4) Quanto costa un biglietto? 5) Dov'è il duomo/la cattedrale? 6) Cerco il centro. 7) Dritto e poi a sinistra. 8) Vedo il parco. 9) Vorrei comprare due biglietti. 10) Due adulti.

Bathrooms

Let's not overlook the obvious. Some vital vocabulary. . . .

bathroom	la toilette	lah twah-<u>leht</u>
	il gabinetto	eel gah-bee-<u>nayt</u>-toh
	il WC	eel vee-<u>chee</u>
	il bagno	eel <u>bahn</u>-nyoh
ladies	signore	seen-<u>nyoh</u>-ray
women's	donna	<u>dohn</u>-nah
gentlemen	signori	seen-<u>nyoh</u>-ree
men's	uomo	<u>woh</u>-moh
toilet paper	la carta igienica	lah <u>kahr</u>-tah ee-<u>jeh</u>- nee-kah

Note: Be careful. *Signore* is *ladies* (plural). It looks identical to *signore* (*gentleman*—singular). The men's room is usually identified with the plural form *signori*.

Culture note—Bathroom fees, toilets and etiquette

Where can you find a bathroom when you're out and about? Public bathrooms are usually marked *toilette* or WC. You can find them most easily in train stations or in bars (you should buy something if you use the bathroom at a bar). You may have to pay for the toilet with a coin, or you may have to buy a token and use the token to enter the bathroom.

The toilet may not have a seat, just a rim. Public bathrooms are frequently out of toilet paper. You will want to carry some extra with you when you go out. The flusher is usually located on the wall above the toilet, either a button or a kind of "rocker," but it could be at knee or floor level.

If an attendant is working in the bathroom, she will expect to be tipped, and it is rude not to leave her some money. (She might even say something to you if you don't.) Don't expect the paper towel dispenser to be stocked, either.

Mail Service

post office	l'ufficio postale	loof-*fee*-choh pohs-*tah*-lay
mailbox	la cassetta delle lettere	lah kahs-*sayt*-tah *dayl*-lay *leht*-tay-ray
letter	la lettera	lah *leht*-tay-rah
stamp	il francobollo	eel *frahn*-koh-*boh*-loh
postcard	la cartolina	lah kahr-toh-*lee*- nah
by airmail	per via aerea	payr *vee*-ah ah-*eh*-ray-ah
to America	a America	ah ah-*may*-ree-kah

Culture note—Mail service

The mail service in Italy is not the fastest or most reliable in the world. Mail your postcards early in your trip. For faster service, visit the post office at the Vatican, which has its own mail system, including its own stamps.

The easiest place to buy stamps in Italy is at a tobacconist's shop. You can certainly buy postage at a post office, as well, but don't expect fast or friendly service.

Culture note—Internet access

If you prefer to contact friends at home via the Internet, you will have many options for doing so in Italy. You can access the Internet in cyber cafes, some laundromats, some hotels—any-place with an "Internet Point" designation. You usually pay for an amount of time up front and receive a username and password so you can log on to an open terminal. Prices are quite reasonable, but connections tend to be slow. Keep an eye on the clock, or you may be cut off mid-message. Also, pay attention to the keyboard. Italian keyboards are slightly different from American ones, and it's easy to type a message that's half gibberish if you don't watch out.

Exchanging Money

money	il denaro	*eel day-<u>nah</u>-roh*
	i soldi	*ee <u>sohl</u>-dee*
currency	la valuta	*lah vah-<u>loo</u>-tah*
cash	i contanti	*ee kohn-<u>tahn</u>-tee*
euro	l'euro	*<u>lay</u>-oo-roh*
to exchange	cambiare	*kahm-<u>byah</u>-ray*
bank	la banca	*lah <u>bahn</u>-kah*
currency exchange	il cambio	*eel <u>kahm</u>-byoh*
ATM	il bancomat	*eel <u>bahn</u>-koh-maht*
cash card	la carta bancomat	*lah <u>kahr</u>-tah <u>bahn</u>-koh-maht*

Culture note—Getting money

With the rapid spread of ATMs, exchanging money is becoming obsolete. It's easier and cheaper to get money from an ATM than to exchange it. If your cash or debit card has a Plus or Cirrus logo on it, just look for an ATM (*un bancomat*) that shows Plus or Cirrus affiliation. You can even find exact locations of compatible machines before you go. (Check with your bank or on the Web.) Make sure you have a four-digit PIN, and know your number rather than an alphabetic equivalent. Italian keypads won't include letters the way American ones do.

You *can* exchange money at banks or at exchange booths in airports or train stations, but bank hours are limited and money changers tend to give bad rates. Also, you pay a fee each time you exchange money, more than the fee for using an ATM. And don't exchange money with a changer in the street. You could be buying counterfeit bills.

For my own peace of mind, I always take along some traveler's checks or cash when I travel abroad, just in case I have trouble withdrawing money. Between credit cards and ATMs, though, I haven't had to exchange money in years. I always bring the cash or the unused traveler's checks home and redeposit them in the bank. You might decide to skip this backup system entirely.

Exercise 5.7

What would you say in the following situations?

1. You're looking for a bathroom.

2. You're looking for an ATM.

3. You need euros.

4. You're looking for a post office.

5. You need stamps to America.

6. You would like to exchange dollars.

Answers: 1) Dov'è la toilette/il gabinetto/il WC, per favore? OR Cerco la toilette . . .. 2) Dov'è un bancomat, per favore? OR Cerco un bancomat. 3) Ho bisogno di euro. 4) Dov'è un ufficio postale, per favore? OR Cerco un ufficio postale. 5) Ho bisogno di francobolli a America. 6) Vorrei cambiare i dollari.

Grammar—Adjective endings, plurals

	Singular	**Plural**
Masculine	il passaport<u>o</u> american<u>o</u>	i passaport<u>i</u> american<u>i</u>
	il ristorant<u>e</u> nuov<u>o</u>	i ristorant<u>i</u> nuov<u>i</u>
Feminine	la camer<u>a</u> liber<u>a</u>	le camer<u>e</u> liber<u>e</u>
	la tavol<u>a</u> nuov<u>a</u>	le tavol<u>e</u> nuov<u>e</u>

One more bit of plural grammar before we end this chapter. To be absolutely correct, any adjectives you use with plural nouns should also be in plural form (and should still match the gender of the noun). Fortunately, that's pretty easy. If the plural noun ends in -i, then the adjective will almost always end in -i, as well. If the plural noun ends in -e, then the adjective usually will, too. (See the table above.)

One exception to this pattern is the ending for adjectives that end in -e in singular form, such as *verde* (green). As you may recall, these adjectives keep their -e ending for masculine or feminine singular nouns. Thus, *il libro verde* (masculine—*the green book*) has the same adjective ending as *la carta verde* (feminine—*the green paper*). The plural ending for these adjectives is also the same for masculine or feminine nouns—the *-e* changes to *-i* (a pattern we have also seen in the noun endings, themselves).

* In other words, if the adjective ends in *-e* (instead of *-o*), then only *-e* for singular, only *-i* for plural.

Culture note—Luggage lockers

If you want to see sights but don't want to haul your baggage with you, you can use the luggage storage (*deposito bagagli*) or luggage lockers (*deposito bagagli automatico*) that are usually available at the train station. Fees are very reasonable. If you deposit your luggage with workers at a counter, make sure you get their hours of operation, so you know when you can reclaim your bags.

Culture note—Petty crime

Violent crime is rare in Italy, but petty crime abounds, especially in cities, around tourist sights, around train and bus stations, and on crowded public transportation. Beware of pickpockets! You will see warnings posted all over—on the Metro, on buses, in train stations, even in churches. *Heed them.*

Be extra alert if a group of children crowds around you or someone comes and holds something (say, a newspaper) in front of you, blocking your view. Both are common distraction techniques used by thieves. Don't get so involved in admiring the sights that you won't notice someone lifting your wallet. Better yet, keep most of your money in a money belt under your clothes. Don't carry a purse or bag slung loosely over your shoulder, where it could easily be snatched away, perhaps by a rider on a motorbike. Don't keep valuables in a backpack or fanny pack that could be slit open and emptied while you are distracted. When in a crowd, be alert, be cautious, be super sensible, even a little suspicious. This is not the time to rely on the honesty of strangers.

6   Arrival and Transportation

Numbers (100-1000, by 100)

Let's take on the last of Italian numbers—hundreds and thousands. Again, review the previous number sections to imprint them a little more deeply in your memory before starting this new section.

100	cento	*chehn-toh*
200	duecento	*doo-ay-chehn-toh*
300	trecento	*tray-chehn-toh*
400	quattrocento	*kwaht-troh-chehn-toh*
500	cinquecento	*cheen-kway-chehn-toh*
600	seicento	*say-ee-chehn-toh*
700	settecento	*say-tay-chehn-toh*
800	ottocento	*oh-toh-chehn-toh*
900	novecento	*noh-vay-chehn-toh*
1.000	mille	*meel-lay*

You now have the building blocks to build numbers up to (and past) one thousand. See how large numbers are put together. Some of these examples have hyphens between different parts of the words to make them easier to read. Correctly written, each Italian number is one long word without breaks.

101	centouno
102	centodue
213	duecento-tredici
1.000	mille
2.000	duemila
3.000	tremila
11.000	undicimila
16.400	sedicimila-quattrocento
21.700	ventunomila-settecento
48.930	quarantottomila-novecento-trenta
50.515	cinquantamila-cinquecento-quindici

Exercise 6.1

Can you write out these numbers in Italian without looking at the list above?

1.	165	7.	328
2.	647	8.	783
3.	812	9.	479
4.	231	10.	1.014
5.	597	11.	3.285
6.	956		

Answers: 1) cento-sessanta-cinque, 2) seicento-quaranta-sette, 3) ottocento-dodici, 4) duecento-trentuno, 5) cinquecento-novanta-sette 6) novecento-cinquanta-sei, 7) trecento-ventotto, 8) settecento-ottanta-tré, 9) quattrocento-settanta-nove, 10) mille-quattordici, 11) tremila-duecento-ottanta-cinque

Reality check: If you really hate learning numbers, you can probably get by just fine without the high numbers. Concentrate on being able to count comfortably from one to twenty and then make do if you need to communicate larger numbers.

Culture note—24-hour clock

Europeans use the 24-hour clock (also known as military time) for official designations of time (for example, on train, bus, or TV schedules) and often in casual usage. If you see a time listed as 20.00, for example, just remember to subtract twelve to get the "regular" time, eight p.m. In conversation, Italian speakers do not always use the 24-hour clock. They differentiate between a.m and p.m. by saying *di mattina* for morning times and *del pomeriggio* for afternoon times. Evening times use *di sera* and night times *di notte*. Note that Italians generally separate the hour and minutes with a period (2.30 del pomeriggio; 9.00 di mattina).

Telling Time

Telling time in a foreign language always seems confusing at first. You might want to familiarize yourself with ways of asking and telling time.

| What time is it? | Che ora è? | *kay oh-rah eh?* |

Hours

one o'clock	l'una	*loo-nah*
It's one o'clock	È l'una.	*eh loo-nah*
for all other hours	Sono le ___	*soh-noh lay ___*
It's seven.	Sono le sette.	*soh-noh lay seht-tay*

Minutes

| and | e | *ay* |
| It's eight twenty-nine (8:29). | Sono le otto e ventinove. | *soh-noh lay oht-toh ay vayn-tee-noh-vay* |

After the ½ hour

| before (the hour) | meno (="minus") | *may-noh* |
| It's five before one p.m. (12:55) | Sono le tredici meno cinque. | *soh-noh lay tray-dee-chee may-noh cheen-kway* |

Up to the ½ hour

and	e	*ay*
quarter	un quarto	*oon kwahr-toh*
It's a quarter after three (3:15).	Sono le tre e un quarto.	*soh-noh lay tray ay oon kwahr-toh*
half	mezzo/a	*mehd-dzoh/-dzah*
It's six-thirty (6:30).	Sono le sei e mezzo.	*soh-noh lay seh-ee ay mehd-dzoh*

If not using the 24-hour clock

in the morning	di mattina	*dee maht-tee-nah*
in the afternoon	del pomeriggio	*dayl poh-may-reed-joh*
in the evening	di sera	*dee say-rah*
at night	di notte	*dee noht-tay*

Other words

noon	il mezzogiorno	*eel mayd-dzoh-johr-noh*
midnight	la mezzanotte	*lah mayd-dzah-noht-tay*
It's noon.	È mezzogiorno.	*eh mayd-dzoh-johr-noh*

Survival Strategy: As a tourist, you will usually only care about opening and closing times, which you will be able to read either on signs or in your guidebook. Save yourself some trouble. Unless you will be setting or keeping appointments, just take a watch along and don't worry about telling time in Italian.

Exercise 6.2

Che ora è? How do you say the following times in Italian?

1. It's one.

2. It's three.

3. It's eight.

4. It's eleven.

5. It's sixteen.

6. It's four p.m.

7. It's seven ten.

8. It's nine twenty.

9. It's one thirty.

10. It's 15 thirty.

11. It's 3:30 p.m.

12. It's two fifteen.

13. It's a quarter to five.

14. It's five to seven.

15. It's midnight.

16. It's noon.

Answers: 1) È l'una. 2) Sono le tre. 3) Sono le otto. 4) Sono le undici. 5) Sono le sedici. 6) Sono le quattro del pomeriggio. 7) Sono le sette e dieci. 8) Sono le nove e venti. 9) È l'una e mezzo. 10) Sono le quindici e mezzo. 11) Sono le tre e mezzo del pomeriggio. 12) Sono le due e un quarto. 13) Sono le cinque meno un quarto. 14) Sono le sette meno cinque. 15) È mezzanotte. 16) È mezzogiorno.

Culture note—Punctuality

In general, Italians are quite punctual, especially in business. When meeting friends, however, it's often all right to be late (up to 20 or 30 minutes). Some young people purposely arrive a little late to look important.

Arrival

Your arrival in Italy will be less confusing if you know what some of the words around you mean. You should be able to recognize these terms when you see them, but you shouldn't need to produce them yourself, unless you want to ask where the information desk or the luggage carousel is.

passport	il passaporto	*eel pahs-sah-pohr-toh*
passport control	il controllo passaporti	*eel kohn-trohl-loh pahs-sah-pohr-tee*
customs	dogana	*doh-gah-nah*
luggage	il bagaglio	*eel bah-gahl-lyoh*
suitcase	la valigia	*lah vah-leej-jah*
information	informazioni	*een-fohr-maht-tsyoh-nee*
"Do you speak English?"	"Parla inglese?"	*pahr-lah een-glay-say?*

Culture note—Taxis

Taxis are very expensive in Italy and difficult to find. It's not common to flag one down as it passes by. Rather, you must usually telephone for one or find one at a station where they wait for customers. Check the main piazza, the train station and major tourist sights. Try to find out in advance (from your airline or hotel desk, perhaps) what the standard fare is in the city or for a particular trip (e.g., from the airport to the city center), because some taxi drivers will try to rip you off. Pay what's on the meter, plus a small tip, up to about 10% of the fare. Rounding up to a convenient figure and telling the driver that amount works well.

The Alphabet

You sometimes need to spell words as a traveler, usually your name. Also, announcements in airports and train stations may include letters identifying locations and flight or train numbers. Consequently, while it's not necessary to be able to say the alphabet forward and backward in Italian, it's not a bad idea to familiarize yourself with it a little bit.

a	ah	**n**	ehn-nay
b	bee	**o**	oh
c	chee	**p**	pee
d	dee	**q**	koo
e	ay	**r**	ehr-ray
f	ayf-fay	**s**	ehs-say
g	jee	**t**	tee
h	ahk-kah	**u**	oo
i	ee	**v**	voo
j	ee loong-ah	**w**	dohp-pyah voo
k	kahp-pah	**x**	eeks
l	ehl-lay	**y**	eep-see-lohn
m	ehm-may	**z**	dzeh-tah

Exercise 6.3

What Italian words do the following series of letters spell?

1. ah / ehl-lay / bee / ay / ehr-ray / jee / oh

2. jee / ee / oh / ehr-ray / ehn-nay / oh

3. pee / ehr-ray / ay / ehn-nay / oh / tee / ah / dzeh-tah / ee / oh / ehn-nay / ay

4. koo / oo / ee / ehn-nay / dee / ee / chee / ee

5. ayf-fay / ah / ehr-ray / ehm-may / ah / chee / ee / ah

6. ee / tee / ah / ehl-lay / ee / ah

7. voo / ah / ehl-lay / ee / jee / ee / ah

8. ah / oo / tee / oh / bee / oo / ehs-say

9. oo / ehs-say / chee / ee / tee / ah

10. jee / ay / ehl-lay / ah / tee / oh

Answers: 1) albergo, 2) giorno, 3) prenotazione, 4) quindici, 5) farmacia, 6) Italia,
7) valigia, 8) autobus, 9) uscita, 10) gelato

Culture note—Strikes

Strikes are common in Italy, particularly in public transportation.
Don't be surprised if you want to take a train, bus or subway
someday and everything is shut down.

Culture note—Public transportation

Italy has an extensive public transportation system. It is reasonably priced, highly used and more than a little chaotic. Buses and
subway trains can be extremely crowded. The practice is to cram
on board if at all possible. Don't bother waiting for another bus
or subway train that has fewer people. The next one will be just as
crowded. Regular trains can also be overfull. Buying a reservation
ahead of time will at least guarantee you a seat.

Culture note—Ticket validation

Always make sure you have a valid ticket to ride public transportation. You usually need to validate your own ticket on subways,
buses and trains. Look for a little box to stick your ticket into
(either at the stop or in the vehicle itself) so your ticket will be
stamped with the date and time. Buses have orange validating machines on the bus and sometimes at the stop. Yellow train ticket
validating machines are located near the entrance to each platform
(look for one attached to the wall right after you enter the boarding hall). You are supposed to validate your own ticket before
boarding the train. Tickets are checked during train trips and may
be checked at any time on other forms of transportation. If you
are caught riding without a valid ticket, you will face a hefty fine.

Transportation

Unless you are with a tour group with all transportation provided, you should be familiar with the most important means of getting around.

taxi	il taxi	*eel <u>tahk</u>-see*
city bus	l'autobus	*<u>low</u>-toh-boos*
town-to-town bus	il pullman	*eel <u>pool</u>-mahn*
entrance	l'ingresso	*leen-<u>grehs</u>-soh*
exit	l'uscita	*loosh-<u>shee</u>-tah*
subway	la metropolitana	*lah may-troh-poh-lee-<u>tah</u>-nah*
train	il treno	*eel <u>treh</u>-noh*
train station	la stazione ferroviaria	*lah staht-<u>tsyoh</u>-nay fayr-roh-<u>vyah</u>-ryah*
platform	il binario	*eel bee-<u>nahr</u>-yoh*
airport	l'aeroporto	*lah-ay-roh-<u>pohr</u>-toh*
airplane	l'aeroplano	*lah-ay-roh-<u>plah</u>-noh*
flight	il volo	*eel <u>voh</u>-loh*
ferry	il traghetto	*eel trah-<u>gayt</u>-toh*
waterbus	il vaporetto	*eel vah-poh-<u>rayt</u>-toh*
ticket	il biglietto	*eel beel-<u>lyayt</u>-toh*
from. . . to	da . . . a	*dah. . . ah*
for ___ people	per ___ persone	*payr ___ payr-<u>soh</u>-nay*

Culture note—Subways

Only Rome, Milan, Naples and Palermo have subway systems, and those are not extensive. (Italy's many archeological sites prohibit extensive excavations.) You buy a flat-fee ticket for the subway, as you would for the bus. Tickets are sold at train stations and tobacconists' shops. Look for *biglietti* signs. The subway itself is marked with an M sign for *Metro* (itself short for *metropolitana*). Feed your ticket through the machine at the turnstile or gate in the subway tunnel. It will shoot out on the other side for you to pick up. And don't forget it—you could be required to show your ticket on the subway train or when you leave the subway.

Exercise 6.4

How can you best get from place to place?

1.	across Rome or Milan (quickly)	A.	l'autobus
2.	in most towns and cities	B.	il traghetto
3.	in Venice	C.	l'aeroplano
4.	Naples to Sicily	D.	la metropolitana
5.	Rome to London	E.	il vaporetto
6.	Rome to Florence	F.	il treno

Anwers: 1) D, 2) A, 3) E, 4) B, 5) C, 6) F

Culture note—Buses

Italy has a highly effective bus system, both city and rural. Both types of buses display their destination at the front of the bus.

You can purchase a city bus ticket at a tobacconist's shop, some newsstands or the bus terminal, but not on the bus. A single ticket is good for about 70 minutes, on more than one bus and possibly the subway. City buses have three doors. The front and back doors are for entering the bus. The middle door is for exiting the bus. Buses are usually so crowded that it's impractical to enter and exit by the designated door. You can do as the locals do and ignore the door signs. Posted bus schedules are usually inaccurate; you shouldn't rely on listed times. As soon as you enter the bus, you must validate your ticket in the orange machine. Don't expect any personal space on buses, and watch out for petty thieves. And you will notice, if you haven't before, that Italians are *not* good at waiting in line. Leave no room between you and the person in front of you if you want to keep your place in line (such as it is).

Pullman are buses that leave the city and connect towns and villages. You buy a bus ticket at the bus station or on the bus itself. Make sure you validate the ticket by stamping it in the machine on the bus. Town-to-town *pullman* leave either around the train station or the city center.

Renting a Car

Travel tip: Should you rent a car or not? If you will be traveling from city to city, you are better off taking the train. If you are going to visit small towns, you can get around on buses. If, however, you intend to visit hard-to-access sights or spend all your time off the beaten path, it might make sense to rent a car. Read the culture note on the next page about driving in Italy before you decide to do so, however.

Reality check: Virtually anyone you would rent a car from is used to dealing with tourists and will be proficient in English. If you would feel better knowing how to rent a car in Italian (just in case), here are some words and phrases to use.

a car	un'auto	*oon ow-toh*
to rent	noleggiare	*noh-layd-djah-ray*
I would like to rent a car.	Vorrei noleggiare un'auto.	*vohr-reh-ee noh-layd-jah-ray oon ow-toh*
I have a reservation.	Ho una prenotazione.	*oh oon-ah pray-noh-taht-tsyoh-nay*
from. . . to	da . . . a	*dah. . . ah*
for ___ people	per ___ persone	*payr ___ payr-soh-nay*
with automatic transmission	con cambio automatico	*kohn kahm-byoh ow-toh-mah-tee-koh*
with air conditioning	con aria condizionata	*kohn ah-ryah kohn-deet-tsyoh-nah-tah*
I need ___.	Ho bisogno di ___.	*oh bee-zohn-nyoh dee ___*
insurance	l'assicurazione	*lahs-see-koo-raht-tsyoh-nay*
driver's license	la patente (di guida)	*lah pah-tehn-tay (dee gwee-dah)*

Travel tips: Make sure you have a decent map (*una cartina stradale*). You should get a map with your rental car, but you may want to bring a good one along with you, if you plan to drive a lot. It's hard enough to find the right roads even with a good map. You don't want to be stuck with a lousy one.

Check your auto insurance policy and your credit cards to see whether they include international auto insurance in their coverage. Your U.S. driver's license is all you need to drive in Italy, but an international driver's license (which includes your license information in multiple languages) is highly recommended. They are available through AAA.

Driving a Car

gas station	la stazione di servizio	*lah stah-tsyoh-nay dee sayr-veet-tsyoh*
Fill it up, please.	Il pieno, per favore.	*eel pyeh-noh, payr fah-voh-ray*
gasoline	la benzina	*lah bayn-dzee-nah*
_(30)_ Liters of gas	_(30)_ litri di benzina	*____ lee-tree dee bayn-dsee-nah*
a self-service station	un distributore automatico	*oon dee-stree-boo-toh-ray ow-toh-mah-tee-koh*
oil	l'olio	*lohl-yoh*
battery	la batteria	*lah baht-tay-ree-ah*
tire	il pneumatico	*eel pnay-oo-mah-tee-koh*
broken	rotto	*roht-toh*
highway	l'autostrada	*low-tohs-trah-dah*
parking lot	un parcheggio	*oon pahr-kayd-joh*
parking meter	un parchimetro	*oon pahr-kee-may-troh*
parking disk	un disco orario	*oon dees-koh oh-rahr-yoh*

Culture note—Driving in Italy

Driving in Italy is not for the faint of heart. Driving can be dangerous. Streets and roads are usually narrow and often winding. Traffic is heavy on main roads and in cities. Traffic jams are common. Yet speed is of the essence to Italian drivers, especially on the *autostrada* (highway—plenty of fatalities there). If you violate Italian traffic rules, you may be fined and have to pay on the spot. Most major highways are toll roads (take a ticket from

continued

the automatic dispenser and keep it to show when you leave the tollway). Gas is expensive, and most gas stations are closed for lunch, closed after 7:30 at night, and closed Sundays and holidays. Cities are filled with one-way streets, road and street signs are terrible (often posted only at the corner, not in advance), and parking is a problem almost everywhere. (Rome is said to have 2 million cars but only 300,000 public parking spaces.) Historic city centers might limit or ban traffic. And renting a car is expensive.

If you decide to drive in Italy, reserve and pay for your car in the U.S. to save money. Get the more easily recognized international driver's license, even though your U.S. license is legally enough. You should learn to drive a stick shift before arriving in Italy, because Italian cars have manual transmission, even most rentals.

Speed limits are marked on road signs; Italians usually ignore them, but tourists should not. Don't drive in the passing lane unless you are actively passing another vehicle, and try to do that quickly. If someone behind you beeps their horn and flashes their headlights, it means they want to pass you. Be wary when someone passes you, however. On two-way roads, they may continue to pass even with oncoming traffic, expecting both outer drivers to edge onto the shoulder, making a temporary third lane in the middle. On any kind of road, they may cut back in front of you with inches to spare.

While many gas stations close for lunch, evenings and holidays, highways have 24-hour service stations. The "Autogrills" are like giant convenience stores and gas stations with impressive fresh buffets. (And wine—but take no chances on alcohol. Italy has very strict drunk driving laws.)

On the main highways, SOS boxes are located every kilometer, each with three buttons, one for police, one for medical, one for gas. In cities, make sure you follow the rules when parking, or you can get a ticket or a boot clamped to your car. To park legally, look for a blue line painted on the ground and parking meters. If you park in a *zona disco*, use a parking disk with a clock face that shows when you arrived.

Culture note—Road signs

Familiarize yourself with the following sign terms, if you will be driving in Italy.

entrata—entrance

incrocio—crossroads

lavori in corso—road work ahead

passaggio a livello—level crossing

pericolo—danger

rallentare—slow down

senso vietato—no entry

senso unico—one way

sosta autorizzata—parking permitted at indicated times

sosta vietata—no parking

strada privata—private road

uscita—exit

vietato l'ingresso—no entry

At the Train Station

The Italian state railway is called *Ferrovie dello Stato*, abbreviated *FS*. Trains are generally reliable, affordable, efficient and far reaching, but are plagued by strikes, are frequently unpunctual, and not always safe.

There are many different types of trains, from superfast ones that require a surcharge to pokey local trains. You can figure out what kind of train you want by looking at the large poster that shows departures (*partenze*) and reading how long it takes to reach your destination. You can buy a train ticket from a travel agent or at the train station, but don't wait until the last minute or you will face a long line. You will need to choose first or second class. If you are taking a popular route or traveling on a weekend or holiday, you will probably want to buy a seat reservation, as well. You should be able to get discounted tickets for children and adults over 65, with children under four riding free. In large stations, you can get train tickets at self-service machines. You can even select and reserve a seat this way. Wherever you buy your ticket, you should double check the date on both your ticket and your seat reservation.

Before you go to the platform (*binario*) to wait for or board your train, check the large, elevated arrival (*arrivi*)/departure (*partenze*) boards that are constantly updated. The trains are listed according to their *final destination*, not by the stops along the way (which may include *your* destination), so make sure you know the final stop of your train or you might miss a change in departure time or platform and then miss the train itself. (Check the large departure schedule posters if you need to find the end city of your train.)

When you arrive on the platform for your train, you should stamp your ticket in the yellow validating machine near the head of the platform. (Look for one mounted on a wall.) Then find the case that displays diagrams of major trains and look for your train. If your train is listed, find the car you want to board, then stand in the area where that car is supposed to stop. Use the letters hanging from the roof above you as guides. Those letters correspond with the letters you will see on the diagram.

Before you board your car, check the destination that is posted on the side of the car next to the door. Not all parts of the train go to the same place, so you want to make sure you board a car that travels to your destination. Note that smoking is no longer allowed on Italian trains.

Culture note—Night trains

Overnight trains can be an efficient way to maximize your time in Italy. You must be vigilant on night trains, however, because they are not always safe. Watch your belongings at all times on a train, but especially on overnight trips.

Grammar—Present tense verb endings, *we*

You already know the verb endings for *io* (I) and *Lei* (you). Now you will see how the verb form for *noi* (we) is formed. You don't have to know the *noi* ("noy") form to travel or visit successfully, but it's fairly easy, and since many people travel with a friend or spouse, it can come in handy. We will look again at the verbs *parlare* (to speak) and *partire* (to leave).

Subject	Verb Ending	Example
io (I)	-o	parl<u>o</u>, part<u>o</u>
Lei (you)	-a/-e	parl<u>a</u>, part<u>e</u>
noi (we)	-iamo	parl<u>iamo</u>, part<u>iamo</u>

Forming the *we* version of Italian verbs is pretty straightforward. You take the stem of the verb (whatever comes before the *-ire, -ere* or *-are* ending when the verb is in its basic, infinitive form) and add the "we" verb ending of *-iamo*. For example, to say "we speak," you take the verb *parlare* and change it to *parliamo*. "We leave" involves changing *partire* to *partiamo*.

As is usually the case, some of the verbs we will want to use the most are irregular and don't quite follow the simple pattern. Here are some common irregular verbs in the "we" form.

avere	essere	potere
(to have)	(to be)	(to be able)
abbiamo	siamo	possiamo

Good news! Some verbs that are irregular in the *io* or *Lei* form, such as *venire* (to come) (*io vengo, Lei viene*), are regular in the *noi* form (*noi veniamo*).

Grammar—"Let's _____!"

The *noi* form of verbs can also be used for suggesting that you and others do something. For example, "Andiamo!" can mean either "We're going!" or "Let's go!", depending on the context.

Exercise 6.5

How would you say the following in Italian? Practice both the *io* form and the *noi* form.

1. I am from _____./We are from _____.
    (io)   Veng_____ da _____.
    (noi)   Ven_____ da _____.
2. My name is_____./Our names our _____.
    (io)   Mi chiam_____ _____.
    (noi)   Ci chiam_____ _____ e

          _____.

3. I have a reservation./We have a reservation.
    (io)   H_____ una prenotazione.
    (noi)   Abb_____ una prenotazione.
4. No, I don't speak Italian./We speak a little Italian.
    (io)   No, non parl_____ italiano.
    (noi)   Parl_____ un po' di italiano.
5. Yes, I'll take the room./No, we won't take it.
    (io)   Sì, prend_____ la camera.
    (noi)   No, non la prend_____.
6. I would like _____./We would like _____.
    (io)   Desider_____ _____.
    (noi)   Desider_____ _____.

Answers: 1) Vengo/Veniamo (dagli Stati Uniti), 2) chiamo/chiamiamo, 3) Ho/Abbiamo, 4) parlo/Parliamo, 5) prendo/prendiamo, 6) Desidero/Desideriamo

---

Culture note—Train toilets

Each train car has bathrooms at the ends of the car. A small sign next to the handle will show whether the room is occupied or vacant, probably by displaying either a red or green color block. Train toilets tend to be rather dirty. Don't use them when the train is in the station, as they flush directly onto the tracks.

7   Emergencies and Additional Vocabulary

Emergencies

Odds are that you won't encounter any emergencies abroad, but if you do, you might not have the time to look up how to say something. Learning some basic emergency vocabulary can be a life-saving investment. If nothing else, at least learn how to say "Help!"

Help!	Aiuto!	*ah-yoo-toh!*
Watch out!	Attenzione!	*ah-tayn-tsyoh-nay!*
Look!	Guardi!	*gwahr-dee!*
Go away!	Se ne vada!	*say nay vah-dah!*
Fire!	Al fuoco!	*ahl foo-oh-koh!*
Call ___!	Chiami ___!	*kyah-mee ___!*
the police	la polizia	*lah poh-leet-tsee-ah*
an ambulance	un'ambulanza	*oon-ahm-boo-lahn-tsah*
the fire department	i pompieri	*ee pohm-pyeh-ree*
a doctor	un medico	*oon meh-dee-koh*
Where is ___?	Dov'è ___?	*doh-veh ___?*
a telephone	un telefono	*oon tay-leh-foh-noh*

Exercise 7.1

How would you say the following in Italian?

1. Call the police!
2. Help!
3. Call an ambulance!
4. Call a doctor!
5. Where is a telephone?
6. Watch out!
7. Fire!
8. I need a doctor!

Answers: 1) Chiami la polizia! 2) Aiuto! 3) Chiami un'ambulanza! 4) Chiami un medico! 5) Dov'è un telefono? 6) Attenzione! 7) Al fuoco! 8) Ho bisogno di un medico!

Culture note—Telephones

The most common telephone you will see in Italy is the cell phone. Italians *love* cells phones. The little "telefonini" are the ultimate in style and self-importance and contribute greatly to that desirable Italian image, the *bella figura*. You will hear the ringing of phones and rapid-fire Italian conversations every-where—on trains, subways, and buses, in museums, stores, restaurants and on the street. The cell phone is a required accessory for fashionable Italians of all ages.

If you need to use a telephone, public phones are available. Most of them take only Italian phone cards for payment, which are available at a tobacconist's shop. In large cities, public phones may also be available at the post office.

A pre-paid U.S. phone card (such as AT&T) can be a familiar way to call home from Italy, though not the cheapest. (You need to use the phone company's *Italian* dial-up number, probably available in the package when you buy the card.) If you have a phone in your hotel room, you can usually use your phone card to call internationally and not pay any sur-charge. People can also call you in your room, usually at no cost to you. Another possibility is buying an Italian cell phone and the minutes to go with it.

So what's the best option? It's hard to predict what the best way of calling home will be. Telecommunications are changing so rapidly that what I have written here could be out of date by the time you intend to travel. A good way to get current information is to check a travel guide book that updates its information annually. I know that the Rick Steves' guide to Italy, for example, includes a good overview of current phone options and costs.

A local phone call is *una telefonata urbana*. A long-distance call is *una telefonata interurbana*. An international call is *una telefonata internazionale*. A busy signal is a series of long "too-too-too" sounds. A ring is a series of short, quick "too-too-too" sounds. People usually answer the phone by saying, *"Pronto!"*

Culture note—Pharmacies

Pharmacies (*farmacie*) in Italy function as mini-clinics. People go there for advice and treatment before visiting a doctor. In addition to medicine and herbal remedies, pharmacies offer pretty much anything that has to do with health or personal hygiene. They are identified by a large green neon cross outside the door.

Pharmacies must be open beyond regular business hours in case of emergency, but do so on a rotating basis. If you need a pharmacy at night, on the weekend or during a holiday, you can find the pharmacies that are on duty by checking the posting at the nearest pharmacy or asking someone for *le farmacie di turno*.

At the doctor / At the pharmacy

No one wants to get sick or hurt while away from home (and if you do, your healthcare worker may know English), but there's peace of mind in knowing some rudimentary health vocabulary.

It hurts here.	Mi fa male qui.	*mee fah <u>mah</u>-lay kwee*
I'm sick.	Mi sento male.	*mee <u>sayn</u>-toh <u>mah</u>-lay*
I have ___.	Ho ___.	*oh ___*
a fever	la febbre	*lah <u>fehb</u>-bray*
constipation	la stitichezza	*lah stee-tee-<u>kayt</u>-tsah*
diarrhea	la diarrea	*lah dee-ahr-<u>reh</u>-ah*
a headache	mal di testa	*mahl dee <u>teh</u>-stah*
a stomach ache	mal di stomaco	*mahl dee <u>stoh</u>-mah-koh*
a cold	il raffreddore	*eel rahf-frayd-<u>doh</u>-ray*
Please write it down.	Lo scriva, per favore.	*loh <u>skree</u>-vah, payr fah-<u>voh</u>-ray*

Note: If you have a chronic health condition, know how to say it in Italian, just as a precaution.

I'm diabetic.	Sono diabetico/a.	*<u>soh</u>-noh dee-ah-<u>beh</u>-tee-koh/-kah*
I have a heart condition.	Ho disturbi cardiaci.	*oh dees-<u>toor</u>-bee kahr-<u>dee</u>-ah-chee*

I have high blood pressure.	Ho la pressione alta.	*oh lah prays-<u>syoh</u>-nay <u>ahl</u>-tah*
I'm allergic to ___.	Sono allergico/a a ___.	*<u>soh</u>-noh ahl-<u>lehr</u>-jee-koh/-kah ah ___*
penicillin	la penicillina	*lah pay-nee-cheel-<u>lee</u>-nah*
peanuts	arachidi	*ah-<u>rah</u>-kee-dee*

Culture note—At the doctor

Many Italian doctors understand English or can at least read it. If you need to visit a doctor (remember to try a pharmacy first, if your condition is not serious), you may want to write down your symptoms.

In the Italian system, doctors expect to be paid in cash at the time of an office visit. If you end up in the hospital emergency room, however, it's possible you won't be charged, as a courtesy to you as a foreigner. If you are concerned about financing medical care, you might ask about religious organizations that offer free medical help.

Body Parts

head	la testa	*lah <u>teh</u>-stah*
face	il viso	*eel <u>vee</u>-zoh*
	la faccia	*lah <u>faht</u>-chah*
ear	l'orecchio	*loh-<u>rayk</u>-kyoh*
eye	l'occhio	*<u>lohk</u>-kyoh*
nose	il naso	*eel <u>nah</u>-soh*
mouth	la bocca	*lah <u>bohk</u>-kah*
tooth	il dente	*eel <u>dehn</u>-tay*
throat	la gola	*lah <u>goh</u>-lah*
neck	il collo	*eel <u>kohl</u>-loh*
shoulder	la spalla	*lah <u>spahl</u>-lah*
chest	il torace	*eel toh-<u>rah</u>-chay*
	il petto	*eel <u>peht</u>-toh*
heart	il cuore	*eel <u>kwoh</u>-ray*
stomach	lo stomaco	*loh <u>stoh</u>-mah-koh*

back	il dorso	eel <u>dohr</u>-soh
	la schiena	lah <u>skyeh</u>-nah
arm	il braccio	eel <u>braht</u>-choh
elbow	il gomito	eel <u>goh</u>-mee-toh
hand	la mano *	lah <u>mah</u>-noh
finger	il dito	eel <u>dee</u>-toh
leg	la gamba	lah <u>gahm</u>-bah
knee	il ginocchio	eel jee-<u>nohk</u>-kyoh
foot	il piede	eel <u>pyeh</u>-day
skin	la pelle	lah <u>pehl</u>-lay

*Exception to the general rule that an -o ending indicates a masculine noun.

Exercise 7.2

Can you match the following English body parts to their related Italian terms? If you have trouble, look at the "hint list" for clues.

back, chest, face, hand, leg, neck, nose, skin, stomach, tooth

1. la mano
2. il collo
3. il naso
4. la gamba
5. il torace

6. lo stomaco
7. il viso
8. il dente
9. la pelle
10. il dorso

(Hint list: manual labor, collar, nasal cavity, nice gams!, thoracic medicine, a pleasing visage, dental work, animal pelt, dorsal fin)

Answers: 1) hand, 2) neck, 3) nose, 4) leg, 5) chest, 6) stomach, 7) face, 8) tooth, 9) skin, 10) back

Medication

prescription	la ricetta	lah ree-<u>cheht</u>-tah
aspirin	l'aspirina	lahs-pee-<u>ree</u>-nah
antacid	l'antiacido	lahn-<u>tyah</u>-chee- doh
decongestant	il decongestio- nante	eel day-kohn-jay- styoh-<u>nahn</u>-tay

antihistamine	l'antistaminico	*lahn-tee-stah-__mee__-nee-koh*
cough syrup	lo sciroppo per la tosse	*loh shee-__rohp__-poh payr lah __tohs__-say*
cough drop	la pasticca per la tosse	*lah pah-__steek__-kah payr lah __tohs__-say*

Travel tips: When traveling abroad, take any medicine in its original container, so customs can identify it. Take extra medicine along as a precaution, along with a copy of your prescription. Know the generic names for your meds, because specific brand names may not be available or recognized.

Culture note—Family

Italians are intensely devoted to their families. Family loyalty is sacred. It's important for families to eat together, to take care of grandparents, and to always support their children, even as adults, if necessary. Extended families visit each other often. Italians are even loyal to their family houses, which are passed down in the same family for generations.

While family is still the cornerstone of Italian society, modern social trends are loosening its traditional role. Many young couples live together without marriage, the national birthrate is extremely low, most women work outside the home, and young people are insisting on more individuality and choice in their lives.

Additional Vocabulary

Travelers frequently want to know how to say things beyond the bare necessities. This section includes three very common topics: family, occupations and the weather.

Family

family	la famiglia	*lah fah-__meel__-lyah*
parents	i genitori	*ee jay-nee-__toh__-ree*
father	il padre	*eel __pah__-dray*

mother	la madre	*lah <u>mah</u>-dray*
son	il figlio	*eel <u>feel</u>-lyoh*
daughter	la figlia	*lah <u>feel</u>-lyah*
husband	il marito	*eel mah-<u>ree</u>-toh*
wife	la moglie	*lah <u>mohl</u>-lyay*
grandparents	i nonni	*ee <u>nohn</u>-nee*
grandmother	la nonna	*lah <u>nohn</u>-nah*
grandfather	il nonno	*eel <u>nohn</u>-noh*
grandchild	il/la nipote	*eel/lah nee-<u>poh</u>-tay*
grandson/grand-daughter	il/la nipote	*eel/lah nee-<u>poh</u>-tay*
man	l'uomo	*loo-<u>woh</u>-moh*
woman	la donna	*lah <u>dohn</u>-nah*
boy	il ragazzo	*eel rah-<u>gah</u>-tsoh*
girl	la ragazza	*lah rah-<u>gah</u>-tsah*
baby boy	il bambino	*eel bahm-<u>bee</u>-noh*
baby girl	la bambina	*lah bahm-<u>bee</u>-nah*
brother	il fratello	*eel frah-<u>tehl</u>-loh*
sister	la sorella	*lah soh-<u>rehl</u>-lah*
uncle	lo zio	*loh <u>tsee</u>-oh*
aunt	la zia	*lah <u>tsee</u>-ah*
cousin (male)	il cugino	*eel koo-<u>jee</u>-noh*
cousin (fem.)	la cugina	*lah koo-<u>jee</u>-nah*
friend (male)	l'amico	*lah-<u>mee</u>-koh*
friend (female)	l'amica	*lah-<u>mee</u>-kah*
boyfriend	il ragazzo	*eel rah-<u>gaht</u>-tsoh*
girlfriend	la ragazza	*lah rah-<u>gaht</u>-tsah*
cat	il gatto	*eel <u>gaht</u>-toh*
dog	il cane	*eel <u>kah</u>-nay*
fish	il pesce	*eel <u>paysh</u>-shay*
I'm ___.	Sono ___.	*<u>soh</u>-noh ___*
married	sposato/-a	*spoh-<u>zah</u>-toh/-tah*
single (man)	celibe	*<u>cheh</u>-lee-bay*
single (woman)	nubile	*<u>noo</u>-bee-lay*
separated	separato/-a	*say-pah-<u>rah</u>-toh/-tah*
divorced	divorziato/-a	*dee-vohr-<u>tsyah</u>-toh/-tah*
widowed	vedovo/-a	*<u>vay</u>-doh-voh/-vah*

Culture note—Friendship

The Italian concept of friendship is different than in America, deeper and more selective. "True friends" are limited in number and are almost as important as family. They provide total support, acceptance and availability. Such friendships grow slowly, last long, and impose deep obligations on both friends. It's possible to have many more good acquaintances than real "friends" in Italy.

Americans can have the same deep relationships, of course, but we tend to bandy the word "friend" about more casually. Be aware of its narrower meaning in Italy. When getting to know people in Italy, don't rush into compliments or criticisms. Diplomacy is highly valued and will make you a more desirable acquaintance and, who knows, perhaps a true friend some day.

Grammar—Third person singular (he/she/it)

The *Lei* form (you) is important to you as a visitor in Italy, because it is the proper way to address most of the people you will speak to in Italian. The *Lei* form offers dividends beyond appropriate and correct speech, however. When you learn the *Lei* form, you get a bonus with it—it's the same verb form you use with *he*, *she* and *it*.

Regular verbs

	-are verbs	**-ere verbs**	**-ire verbs**
I (io)	-o	-o	-o
you (Lei)	-a	-e	-e
he/she/it*	-a	-e	-e

	parlare (to speak)	vedere (to see)	partire (to leave)
I (io)	parlo	vedo	parto
you (Lei)	parla	vede	parte
he/she/it*	parla	vede	parte

* There are multiple ways to say he/she/it. It's much easier to take advantage of Italian's flexible pronoun system and just leave the he/she/it out, as Italians usually do. If you are really motivated and want to learn pronouns, you can get by most of the time with the following: *lui* (he), *lei* (she), *esso* (it—masculine), *essa* (it—feminine).

Some irregular verbs

	avere (to have)	essere (to be)
I (io)	ho	sono
you (Lei)	ha	è
he/she/it	ha	è

Exercise 7.3
How would you answer these questions in Italian?

1. É sposato/-a?
2. Come si chiama il marito/la moglie?
3. Ha figli?
4. Ha nipoti?

Answers: 1) Si, sono sposato/-a. OR No, non sono sposato/-a. 2) Si chiama ____. 3) Si, ho ____. OR No, non ho figli. 4) Si, ho ____. OR No, non ho nipoti.

Occupations

Remember, it is considered ill-mannered to ask strangers or new acquaintances about their occupations. At some point, however, the topic may come up. If someone asks you about your job, then you can talk about it and ask about theirs without fear of offense.

What do you do?	Che cosa fa?	kay koh-sah fah?
I'm a(n) ____.	Sono ____.	soh-noh ____
My wife is ____.	Mia moglie è ____.	mee-ah mohl-lyay eh
My husband is ____.	Mio marito è ____.	mee-oh mah-ree-toh eh
accountant	ragioniere/-a	rah-joh-nyeh-ray/-rah
architect	architetto	ahr-kee-tayt-toh

artist	artista	*ahr-tee-stah*
businessman	uomo d'affari	*woh-moh dahf-fah-ray*
businesswoman	donna d'affari	*dohn-nah dahf-fah-ray*
carpenter	carpentiere	*kahr-payn-tyeh-ray*
computer programmer	programmatore/-trice di computer	*proh-grahm-mah-toh-ray/-tree-chay dee kum-pyoo-tur*
doctor	medico/-a	*meh-dee-koh/-kah*
engineer	ingegnere	*een-jayn-nyeh-ray*
farmer	agricoltore	*ah-gree-kohl-toh-ray*
housewife	casalinga	*kah-sah-leen-gah*
laborer	manovale	*mah-noh-vah-lay*
lawyer	avvocato	*ahv-voh-kah-toh*
manager	direttore	*dee-rayt-toh-ray*
mechanic	meccanico	*mayk-kah-nee-koh*
minister	pastore	*pahs-toh-ray*
musician	musicista	*moo-zee-chee-stah*
nun	suora	*swoh-rah*
nurse	infermiere/-a	*een-fayr-myeh-ray/-rah*
pilot	pilota	*pee-loh-tah*
plumber	idraulico	*ee-draw-lee-koh*
priest	prete	*preh-tay*
professor	professore/-essa	*proh-fays-soh-ray/-rays-sah*
retired	in pensione	*een payn-syoh-nay*
salesperson	commesso/-a	*kohm-mays-soh/-sah*
sales representative	rappresentante di commercio	*rahp-pray-zayn-tahn-tay dee kohm-mehrt-choh*
scientist	scienziato/-a	*shayn-tsyah-toh/-tah*
secretary	segretario/-a	*say-gray-tahr-yoh/-yah*
student	studente/-essa	*stoo-dehn-tay/-tays-sah*
teacher	insegnante	*een-sayn-nyahn-tay*
writer	scrittore/-trice	*skreet-tohr-ay/-tree-chay*
unemployed	disoccupato/-a	*deez-ohk-koo-pah-toh/-tah*
I'm self-employed.	Lavoro in proprio.	*lah-voh-roh een proh-pyoh*

Culture note—Il campanilismo

Traditionally, Italians are fiercely loyal to their village or birthplace, a loyalty second in importance only to family loyalty. In fact, the village is seen as a kind of extended family. *Il campanilismo* (encompassing all within the sound of the village campanile bells) is an intense local loyalty, affection and pride. Villages across Italy have their own unique festivals to celebrate their independent history and heritage.

Culture note—The Mafia

Despite Italy's ongoing fight against corruption, the Mafia still exists, especially in the south. It's not a centralized organization, but territorial. Most Mafia crimes are petty thefts. Be on your toes in crowded situations and you should have no troubles. (And don't leave valuables in your car or unsecured in your room.) Remember, the Mafia is a taboo subject in Italy. You will offend people if you ask or talk about it.

Grammar—Possessive adjectives

When talking about your family, you often want to use a possessive, usually *my* or *our*, to identify your relatives. ("My brother lives in Pisa." "Our daughter is a scientist.") Or you may hear others talking about possession and will want to understand what they are saying. ("May I have your passport?" "Where is your luggage?") Let's look at how to form possessives in Italian.

Definite article + possessive adjective

	M, sing.	**F, sing.**	**M, plural**	**F, plural**
my	il mio	la mia	i miei*	le mie
your/her/his/its	il suo	la sua	i suoi*	le sue
our	il nostro	la nostra	i nostri	le nostre

*irregular forms, must be memorized

As usual, we will discuss just the Italian forms you are most likely to use or encounter: *my*, *your* and *our*. Because the *your* (formal, singular) form is the same as the *her*, *his*, *its* form, we will list those, as well. The base form for *my* is *mio*. The base form for *you* (and *her*/*his*/*its*) is *suo*. And the base form for *our* is *nostro*.

This being Italian, you know things have to get more complicated, and they do. These possessive words are a kind of adjective (telling us something about the noun. *Whose* brother? *My* brother.) and that means that in Italian their endings change just as other adjective endings do. Remember, "the red book" is *il libro rosso* but "the red paper" is *la carta rossa*. (You may want to review adjective endings on page 115.) As you can see on the table above, the masculine singular ending is -*o* (*mio, suo, nostro*) and the feminine singular ending is -*a* (*mia, sua, nostra*). That looks familiar, doesn't it? Those are our "default" masculine and feminine endings. It's not too big a leap, then, to figure out that "my sister" would be *mia sorella* and "our son" would be *nostro figlio*, or, switching them around, "our sister" is *nostra sorella* and "my son" is *mio figlio*. The gender of the noun determines the ending of the possessive adjective.

But what's the deal with the *il*s and *la*s in that table? OK, I have to confess. I've been using simplified examples, so far. Most of the time, you use possessive adjectives in Italian (the *mio*/*sua* part) along *with* the definite article (the *il*/*la* part). (You get to skip the definite article sometimes if you are talking about family members in the singular.) That means that to identify a book as yours, you would call it *il mio libro*. If someone asks you for your passport, it will be *il suo passaporto*.

If you turn to the plural forms of the possessive words, you can see that the "default" endings also hold true for them. While masculine singular ends in -*o*, masculine plural ends in -*i*. Feminine singular ends in -*a*, but feminine plural ends in -*e*. Using our examples from above, "my sister" changes from singular *(la) mia sorella* to plural *le mie sorelle* and "our son" changes from singular *(il) nostro figlio* to plural *i nostri figli*. As you can see, with plural nouns the definite article also needs to be plural. "My books" would be *i miei libri*; "his ties" would be *le sue cravatte*.

In closing, there is a reason possessive adjectives are introduced at the end of this book. You will want to be aware of them, but it's unlikely they are a priority for you to master.

Culture note—Italian weather

The weather in Italy varies greatly from the mountainous north to the coastal south. In winter, rain is frequent throughout most of the country, with snow in the mountains. In summer, temperatures can be pleasant in the mountains but scorching almost everywhere else. Veteran travelers recommend visiting Italy during the "shoulder seasons," the pleasant months of April, May, September and October, when tourist crowds are also thinner. August is not only unbearably hot, but most Italians depart on their own vacations, leaving behind virtual ghost towns in some cases.

Weather

weather	il tempo	*eel tehm-poh*
How is the weather?	Che tempo fa?	*kay tehm-poh fah?*
It's ___.	Fa ___.	*fah ___.*
good weather	bel tempo	*behl tehm-poh*
bad weather	cattivo tempo	*kaht-tee-voh tehm-poh*
cold	freddo	*frayd-doh*
cool	fresco	*fray-skoh*
hot	caldo	*kahl-doh*
It's ___.	È ___.	*eh ___*
cloudy	nuvoloso	*noo-voh-loh-soh*
windy	ventoso	*vayn-toh-soh*
foggy	nebbioso	*nayb-byoh-soh*

It's sunny.	C'è il sole.	*chay eel soh-lay*
It's raining	Piove.	*pyoh-vay*
It's snowing.	Nevica.	*nay-vee-kah*

Culture note—Celsius

Remember that Italy uses the Celsius temperature scale. Water freezes at 0 degrees Celsius and boils at 100 degrees. Twenty degrees Celsius is the quite pleasant temperature of 68 degrees Fahrenheit, while 32 degrees Celsius is a steamy 90 in Fahrenheit.

For a rough conversion of Celsius temperatures to Fahrenheit, double the Celsius number and add 30. For example, start with 20 degrees Celsius, double it to 40, add 30 for 70, which gets you close to the correct Fahrenheit reading of 68. While it's not perfect, this shortcut will at least get you in the ballpark.

$$\text{Celsius reading} \times 2, + 30 =$$
$$\text{approximate Fahrenheit reading}$$

If you have time or need a very accurate conversion, you can always check the temperature on a conversion chart. Here is an abbreviated version of one.

Temperature Conversion Chart

C	F
40	104
35	95
30	86
25	77
20	68
15	59
10	50
5	41
0	32
-10	14
-20	-4

Exercise 7.4

What do you need to prepare yourself for the following weather conditions? Match the listings in columns A and B.

A	B
1. Fa fresco.	A. costume da bagno o shorts
2. Piove.	
3. C'è il sole.	B. cappello o occhiali da sole
4. Fa freddo e nevica.	C. giacca o maglione
5. Fa caldo.	D. ombrello
	E. cappotto e guanti

Answers: 1) C, 2) D, 3) B, 4) E, 5) A

Culture note—Umbrellas

If you forget to bring an umbrella to Italy (or purposely leave yours behind to save luggage space), don't worry about it. Street vendors will materialize from nowhere at the first drops of rain, trying to sell you an umbrella.

If you enter a restaurant from the rain, look around the entrance for some sort of stand, pail or bin to stash your wet umbrella in. The owners will appreciate it if you don't let your umbrella drip all over the floor.

A final word

That's it! You have covered the basics of Italian that will serve you well as a visitor in that glorious country. You have learned a little grammar, quite a bit of vocabulary, and a lot about Italian social customs. Congratulations! Whatever effort you were able to put into your preparation will pay off handsomely in Italy. You *will* be able to communicate with Italians, understand much of what is going on around you, and experience daily life without the paralyzing fear of complete uncertainty. So dive in and enjoy your Italian visit!

And then tell me about it. Please. The good, the bad, what you learned, what surprised you. I would love to hear about your experiences with this book and in Italy. Write me care of World Prospect Press, PO Box 100, Shell Rock, IA 50670 (on the Web at worldprospect.com), or you can reach me via fax (319-885-4160) or e-mail (bingham@worldprospect.com). **Your stories could even be included in an upcoming book—check out pages 189-190 for more information.**

Have a great trip, and I look forward to hearing from you!

Self-Test

Can you remember what to expect and how to communicate in the following situations? Test yourself, then review what you need to work on.

- ❏ Greetings
    - most of the day
    - evening and night
    - informal
- ❏ Introductions
    - introduce yourself
    - ask others their names
- ❏ Origins
    - say where you are from
    - ask others where they are from
- ❏ Leave-taking
    - during most of the day
    - informal
    - on going to bed
- ❏ Manners
    - please
    - thank you
    - you're welcome
    - excuse me
    - That's OK
- ❏ Useful expressions
    - yes/no/and/or
    - "I don't understand."
    - "Please repeat."
    - "Please speak more slowly/loudly."
- ❏ Numbers 0-10
- ❏ Concrete vocabulary
    - identify items in the room around you
- ❏ Days of the week
- ❏ Times of day
    - morning
    - noon
    - afternoon
    - evening
    - night/midnight

❑   Months
❑   Lodging
    "Where is a hotel, please?"
    "Do you have rooms available?"
    "I would like a double room."
    with a shower
    for three nights
    "How much does that cost?"
    "Do you have something cheaper?"
    "I'll take it."
❑   Directions
    there
    right
    left
    straight ahead
❑   Numbers 11-20
❑   Eating out
    meals
    seating customs
    how to order
    some foods and drinks
    how to pay, tip
    "Check, please!"
❑   Numbers 10-100, by ten
❑   Shopping
    "Do you have _____?"
    "I would like. . ."
    types of stores
    clothing
    colors
    miscellaneous items
❑   Numbers 21-99
❑   Units of time
❑   Sightseeing
    places to visit
❑   Rest rooms
    "bathroom"
    men's
    ladies'

❑ Mailing letters
    post office
    stamps
    by airmail
    to America
❑ Exchanging money
    "I would like to exchange money."
    "Where's an ATM?"
❑ Numbers 100-1000, by 100
❑ Telling time
    "When is _____?"
    "It's ten-thirty."
    "It's two-fifteen."
❑ Arrival
    passport control
    information
❑ Alphabet
❑ Transportation
    public transportation
    renting and driving a car
    at the train station
❑ Emergencies
    "Help!"
    "Watch out!"
    "Call a doctor!"
    "Fire!"
    "Where's a telephone?"
❑ At the doctor/pharmacy
    "It hurts here."
    body parts
❑ Medication
❑ Family and occupations
    tell what you have for family and occupations
❑ Weather
    "Che tempo fa?"
    Celsius temperature readings

Remember, there's still more to this book! You have a **Resource Guide** to help you find more useful books, an **Italian-English Dictionary**, and an **English-Italian Dictionary**.

Resource Guide

Italian Culture Guides

Culture Shock! Italy: A Guide to Customs and Etiquette, by Raymond Flower and Alessandro Falassi, Graphic Arts Center Publishing Co., 1995, ISBNs 1558681655/978 1558681651, $12.95

Italian Way, The: Aspects of Behavior, Attitudes, and Customs of the Italians, by Mario Costantino and Lawrence Gambella, Passport Books, 1996, ISBNs 0844280720/978-0844280721, $12.95

Living & Working in Italy, 2nd ed., by Amanda Hinton, How To Books, 2000, ISBNs 1857035003/978-1857035001, $14.95

Living, Studying, and Working in Italy: Everything You Need to Know to Fulfill Your Dreams of Living Abroad, by Travis Neighbor and Monica Larner, Owl Books, 1998, ISBNs 0805051023/978-0805051025, $16.00

Passport Italy: Your Pocket Guide to Italian Business, Customs & Etiquette, by Claudia Gioseffi, World Trade Press, 1997, ISBNs 1885073348/978-1885073341, $6.95

Teach Yourself Italian Language, Life & Culture, by Derek Aust with Mike Zollo, NTC Publishing Group, 2000, ISBNs 0658008978/978-0658008979, $12.95

Compact Dictionaries

Collins Gem Italian Dictionary: Italian-English/English-Italian, 2005, ISBNs 0007126247/978-0007126248, 640 pp., 4.2 x 3.2 x 1.5 inches, $6.95

Insight Travel Dictionary: Italian, 2001, ISBNs 1585730734/978-1585730735, 256 pp., 4 x 2.7 x .6 inches, $5.95

Langenscheidt Universal Italian Dictionary: Italian-English, English-Italian, 2005, ISBNs 1585734918/978-1585734917, 640 pp., 3.9 x 3 x 1.1 inches, $7.95

Larousse Mini Dictionary, Italian-English, English-Italian, 2006, ISBNs 2035421578/978-2035421579, 318 pp., 4.5 x 3.1 x 1.3 inches, $5.95

Phrase Books

Barron's Italian at a Glance, 4th ed., Barron's Educational Series, 2003, ISBNs 0764125133/978-0764125133, 336 pp., 6 x 4.1 x .6 inches, $6.95

Berlitz Italian Phrase Book and Dictionary, Berlitz Travel Guide, 2003, ISBNs 2831578442/978-2831578446, 224 pp., 5.7 x 4 x .4 inches, $8.95

Jiffy Phrasebook Italian, Langenscheidt, 1986, ISBNs 0887299539/978-0887299537, 256 pp., 6.1 x 3.8 x .7 inches, $7.95

Italian, 2nd ed., Lonely Planet, 2003, ISBNs 1864503173/978-1864503173, 256 pp., 5.5 x 3.7 x .6 inches, $7.99

Italian for Travelers, Fodor's Living Language, 1989, ISBNs 1400014905/978-1400014903, 288 pp., 6.8 x 3.9 x .8 inches, $8.95

Italian Phrase Book, DK Eyewitness Travel Guides, 2003, ISBNs 0789494892/978-0789494894, 144 pp., 5.8 x 4.1 x .4 inches, $7.00

Rick Steves' Italian Phrase Book and Dictionary, by Rick Steves, Avalon Travel Publishing, 2003, ISBNs 1566915201/978-1566915205, 224 pp., 6 x 3.9 x 7 inches, $7.95

Italian-English Dictionary

How to use this dictionary

The purpose of this dictionary is to help you decipher written and spoken Italian. Because you will be exposed to more Italian than you will need to produce, this dictionary contains more entries than the English-Italian dictionary that follows it. It is by no means comprehensive, however.

Italian words are listed in bold. Verbs are listed in the infinitive form, as well as separate listings for some common inflected forms. Nouns are listed in singular form, followed by the definite article and, if necessary, *m* or *f* to show whether the noun is masculine or feminine. Plural forms of many nouns are noted in parentheses. Adjectives are listed in their masculine forms with alternate feminine endings. Pronunciations are not located here but are included in the English-Italian dictionary.

a until, to
abbacchio, l' *m* roast lamb
abbacchio alla scottadita, l' *m* grilled lamb cutlets
abbastanza enough
abbiamo we have
abbigliamento, l' *m* clothing
abboccato/a medium sweet, semi-dry
abruzzese, all' with red peppers and possibly ham
acciuga, l' *f* (le acciughe) anchovy
aceto, l' *m* vinegar
acetosella, l' *f* sorrel
acido/a sour, tart
acqua, l' *f* (le acque) water
acquacotta, l' *f* soup of bread/vegetables, possibly egg/cheese also
acqua del rubinetto, l' *f* tap water
acqua di seltz, l' *f* seltzer water
acqua minerale, l' *f* mineral water
acqua tonica, l' *f* tonic water
adulto/a, l'/l' *m/f* (gli adulti/le adulte) adult
aerea, via via air mail

aeroplano, l' *m* (gli aeroplani) airplane
aeroporto, l' *m* (gli aeroporti) airport
affettato, l' *m* (gli affettati) sliced salami or ham
affogato poached (egg)
affumicato/a smoked
aglio, l' *m* garlic
agnello, l' *m* (gli angelli) lamb
agnello abbacchio, l' *m* very young lamb
agosto August
agricoltore, l' *m* (gli agricoltori) farmer
agro, all' lemon juice/oil dressing
agrodolce, l' *m* sweet and sour sauce
aiutare to help
aiuto! Help!
al with, in the style of
ala, l' *f* (le ali) wing
albergo, l' *m* (gli alberghi) hotel
albicocca, l' *f* (le albicocche) apricot
alfabeto, l' *m* alphabet
alfredo dairy sauce
alice, l' *f* (le alici) anchovy

alimentari, il **negozio di** grocery store

all'/alla with, in the style of

allergico/a allergic

allodola, l' *f* (le allodole) lark (bird)

alloro, l' *m* bay leaf

alto/a high

amabile slightly sweet (wine)

amaretto, l' *m* almond-flavored liqueur

amaro/a bitter

amaro, l' *m* (gli amari) after-dinner drink, bitters

amatriciana sauce of bacon, tomatoes, hot pepper

ambulanza, l' *f* (le ambulanze) ambulance

America, l' *f* America

americano (aperitif) vermouth, bitters, brandy, lemon peel

amico/a, l'/l' *m/f* (gli amici/le amiche) friend

analcolico/a non-alcolholic

ananas, l' *m* pineapple

anatra, l' *f* (le anatre) duck

anche also

andare to go

andata, l' *f* (le andate) outward journey

andata, di sola one-way (ticket)

andata e ritorno round trip

andiamo we go

anello, l' *m* (gli anelli) small pasta ring

anguilla, l' *f* (le anguille) eel

anguria, l' *f* (le angurie) watermelon (north)

animale, l' *m* (gli animali) animal

animale domestico, l' *m* pet

anitra, l' *f* (le anitre) duck

anno, l' *m* (gli anni) year

antiacido, l' *m* (gli antiacidi) antacid

antipasto, l' *m* (gli antipasti) appetizer

antipasti a scelta appetizers of one's choice

antipasti assortiti assorted appetizers

antipasti di mare seafood appetizers

antistaminico, l' *m* (gli antistaminici) antihistamine

aperitivo, l' *m* (gli aperitivi) aperitif

Aperol (aperitif) bitters, non-alcoholic

aperto/a open

appetito, l' *m* (gli appetiti) appetite

aprile April

arachide, l' *f* (le arachidi) peanut

aragosta, l' *f* (le aragoste) lobster

arancia, l' *f* (le arance) orange

aranciata orangeade

arancini Italian rice snacks

arancione orange (color)

architetto, l' *m* (gli architetti) architect

argenteo/a silver (color)

argento, l' *m* silver (metal)

aria condizionata, l' *f* air conditioning

aringa, l' *f* (le aringhe) herring

arista, l' *f* (le ariste) pork loin

arista alla fiorentina pork roast with garlic, rosemary, cloves

arrivederci goodbye

arrivo, l' *m* (gli arrivi) arrival

arrosto/a roasted

arsella, l' *f* (le arselle) scallop

artista, l'/l' *m/f* (gli artisti/le artiste) artist

asparago, l' *m* (gli asparagi) asparagus

asparagi alla fiorentina asparagus with fried eggs/cheese

aspirina, l' *f* (le aspirine) aspirin

assegno turistico, l' *m* (gli assegni turistici) traveler's check

assicurazione, l' *f* insurance

assortito/a assorted

astice, l' *m* (gli astici) lobster

attento! careful!

attenzione! attention!, careful!

attesa: 20 minuti waiting time: 20 minutes

Austria, l' *f* Austria

auto, l' *f* (le auto) car

autobus, l' *m* (gli autobus) city bus

autogrill, l' *m* (gli autogrill) roadside restaurant

automatico/a automatic

autostrada, l' *f* (le autostrade) highway

autunno, l' *m* (gli autunni) fall, autumn

avanti   ahead, forward

avere   to have

avvocato, l' *m* (gli avvocati) lawyer

baccalà, il (i baccalà) dried salt cod

baccalà alla romana   dried salt cod with tomato sauce, garlic, parsley

baccalà alla vicentina   dried salt cod cooked in milk

bagaglio, il (i bagagli) luggage

bagno, il (i bagni) bath, bathroom

bambino/a, il/la (i bambini/le bambine) baby, child, boy/girl

banana, la (le banane) banana

banca, la (le banche) bank

banco, il (i banchi) bank; seat, bench

Bancomat, il   automated banking, ATM, cash machine

bar, il (i bar) bar, cafè

barba, la (le barbe) beard

barbabietola, la (le barbabietole) beet

barbiere, il (i barbieri) barber

basilico, il   basil

batteria, la (le batterie) battery

beige   beige

bello/a   nice, beautiful, pretty

ben cotta/o   well done (meat)

bene   good, well

benzina, la   gasoline

benvenuto/a/i/e   welcome

bere   to drink

bevanda, la (le bevande) drink, beverage

bianco/a   white

bibita frizzante, la (le bibite frizzanti) soda pop, soft drink

bicchiere, il (i bicchieri) glass

bicicletta, la (le biciclette) bicycle

biglietto, il (i biglietti) ticket

binario, il (i binari) train platform

biondo/a   fair, blond, light (beer)

birra, la (le birre) beer

birra rossa, la   dark beer

biscotto, il (i biscotti) cookie

bisogno, il (i bisogni) need

bistecca, la (le bistecche) steak

bistecca alla fiorentina, la   grilled steak with pepper, lemon juice, parsley

bistecca di cinghiale, la   wild boar in sweet/sour sauce

bistecca di filetto, la   rib steak

blu   blue

bocca, la (le bocche) mouth

bollito/a   boiled

bollito misto, il   sausages and other boiled meats

bologna, la   mild, smooth sausage

bolognese   sauch of tomatoes, meat, onions, herbs

borsetta, la (le borsette) handbag, purse

bottiglia, la (le bottiglie) bottle

braccio, il (le braccia) arm

braciola, la (le braciole) chop, steak

branzino, il (i branzini) bass (fish)

brasato/a   braised

briciolata   toasted breadcrumbs; sauce of olive oil, black pepper, toasted breadcrumbs

broccolo, il (i broccoli) broccoli

broccoli alla romana   broccoli cooked in olive oil and wine

brodo, il (i brodi) broth, bouillon, soup

brodo di manzo, il   beef broth

brodo di pollo, il   chicken broth

bruidda, la   fish soup

brutto/a   bad, ugly

budino, il (i budini) pudding

buono/a   good

burro, il   butter

busecca, la   tripe, bean, vegetable soup

cacciagione, la   game (food)

cacciatora, alla   cooked with white wine, garlic, rosemary, anchovy paste, hot peppers

cacciucco, il   spiced fish soup

cachi, il (i cachi) persimmon

caffè, il (i caffi) coffee, coffee shop (with coffee, alcohol, maybe some food)

caffè freddo, il   iced coffee

calamaretto, il (i calamaretti) baby squid

calamaro, il (i calamari) squid

caldo/a   hot, warm

calzino, il (i calzini) sock

calzone, il (i calzoni) savory turnover
made with pizza dough
cambiare to exchange
cambio, il (i cambi) exchange,
change; currency exchange office
cambio automatico, il automatic
transmission
camera, la (le camere) room
camera doppia, la (le camere doppie)
double room
cameriera, la (le cameriere) waitress
cameriere, il (i camerieri) waiter
camicetta, la (le camicette) blouse
camicia, la (le camicie) shirt
camicia, in poached (egg)
Campari bitters with orange peel,
herbs
Canada, il Canada
cane, il (i cani) dog
cannella, la cinnamon
cannelloni, i dough tubes filled with
meat, vegetables or cheese, baked in
a white sauce
cannolo, il (i cannoli) cream horn
capire to understand
capisco I understand
cappelletti, i ring-shaped ravioli
stuffed with meat
cappello, il (i cappelli) hat
cappero, il (i capperi) caper
cappone, il (i capponi) capon
cappotto, il (i cappotti) coat, overcoat
cappuccino, il (i cappuccini)
cappuccino
capretto, il (i capretti) kid goat
capricciosa, la cook's specialty pizza
caraffa, la (le caraffe) carafe
caramella, la (le caramelle) candy
carbonara sauce of cheese, eggs,
olive oil, ham
carciofi alla giudea, i deep-fried
artichoke
carciofi alla romana, i cooked
artichokes stuffed with garlic, salt,
olive oil, mint, parsley
carciofo, il (i carciofi) artichoke
carne, la meat
carne ai ferri, la grilled meat
caro/a expensive
carota, la (le carote) carrot

carpa, la (le carpe) carp
carpentiere, il (i carpentieri)
carpenter
carrettiera sauce of tuna, mushroom,
tomato, pepper
carrettiera, alla with hot peppers,
pork
carta, la (le carte) card, map, paper
carta bancomat, la ATM card
carta da lettere, la writing paper
carta di credito, la credit card
carta d'identità, la identity card
carta igienica, la toilet paper
cartolina, la (le cartoline) postcard
casa, la (le case) house
casalinga, la (le casalinghe)
housewife
cassa, la (le casse) cash register
cassata siciliana, la sponge cake with
sweet cream cheese, chocolate,
candied fruit
cassetta delle lettere, la (le cassette)
mailbox
castagna, la (le castagne) chestnut
castagnaccio, il (i castagnacci)
chestnut cake
castello, il (i castelli) castle
cattedrale, la (le cattedrali) cathedral
cattivo/a bad
caviale, il caviar
cavolfiore, il (i cavolfiori) cauliflower
cavolino di Bruxelles, il (i cavolini)
Brussels sprout
cavolo, il (i cavoli) cabbage
c'è there is (=there exists)
cece, il (i ceci) chickpeas
celibe, il (i celibi) single man
cena, la (le cene) dinner, supper
cento hundred
centro, il (i centri) center
centro della città, il center of town,
downtown
cerca you look for
cercare to look for
cerchiamo we look for
cerco I look for
cereali, i cereal
cervello, il (i cervelli) brain
cervo, il (i cervi) deer

cestino per la cartaccia, il (i cestini) wastebasket

cetriolino, il (i cetriolini) pickle

cetriolo, il (i cetrioli) cucumber

che who, which, that, what

chi who

chiamare to call

chiami! call!

Chianti robust red wine of Tuscany

chiaro/a clear, light colored

chiave, la (le chiavi) key

chiesa, la (le chiese) church

chiodo di garofano, il (i chiodi) clove

chiuso/a closed

ciao hi, bye

cicoria, la chicory

ciliegia, la (le ciliege) cherry

cima alla genovese, la veal roll filled with sausage, eggs, mushrooms

cima genovese, la cold veal roll filled with calf's brains, onions, herbs

cinghiale, il (i cinghiali) wild boar

cinquanta fifty

cinque five

cinquecento five hundred

cioccolata, la chocolate

cioccolata calda, la hot chocolate

cipolla, la (le cipolle) onion

cipollina, la (le cipolline) spring onion

ci sono there are, there exist

città, la (le città) city

clementina, la (le clementine) clementine orange

cocomero, il (i cocomeri) watermelon (south)

colazione, la (le colazioni) breakfast

collo, il neck

colore, il (i colori) color

coltello, il (i coltelli) knife

come how

cominciare to begin

commesso/a, il/la (i commessi/le commesse) salesperson

compleanno, il birthday

completo/a full

con with

conchiglia, la (le conchiglie) pasta shell

coniglio, il (i conigli) rabbit

consigliare to recommend

contanti, in (pay) with cash

conto, il (i conti) bill, check

contorno, il (i contorni) side order of vegetables

contro against

controllo passaporti, il passport control

coperto, il (i coperti) cover

coperto, il prezzo del cover charge

copertura, la (le coperture) covering

coppa, la (le coppe) large pork sausage

cornetto, il (i cornetti) croissant, cone

cosa, la (le cose) thing

cosciotto, il (i cosciotti) leg

costare to cost

costata al prosciutto, la (le costate) stuffed chop

costola, la (le costole) rib

costume da bagno, il (i costumi) bathing suit, bathing trunks

cotoletta alla milanese, la (le cotolette) breaded veal cutlet with cheese

cotto/a cooked

cotto a vapore steamed

cozza, la (le cozze) mussels

cravatta, la (le cravatte) necktie

crema, la (le creme) cream, custard, cream soup

crema da barba, la shaving cream

crema di legumi, la vegetable cream soup

crema solare, la suntan cream

crema solare protettiva, la sunscreen

crostaceo, il (i crostacei) shellfish

crostata, la (le crostate) pie, tart

crudo/a rare (meat)

cucchiaio, il (i cucchiai) spoon

cucina tradizionale, la traditional cooking

cugino/a, il/la (i cugini/le cugine) cousin

cumino, il cumin

cuore, il (i cuori) heart

cuscus, il couscous

Cynar aperitif made from artichokes

da from
data, la (le date) date
decongestionante, il decongestant
debole weak
del pomeriggio in the afternoon
denaro, il money
dente, il (i denti) tooth
dentifricio, il (i dentifrici) toothpaste
deodorante, il (i deodoranti)
    deodorant
desidero I would like
destra right
di of
diabetico/a diabetic
diarrea, la diarrhea
dicembre December
diciannove nineteen
diciassette seventeen
diciotto eighteen
dieci ten
digestivo, il (i digestivi) after-dinner
    drink
dio, il (gli dei) God, god
direttore, il (i direttori) manager
disco orario, il (i dischi orari) parking
    disk
disoccupato/a unemployed
distributore automatico, il self-
    service station
disturbi cardiaci, i heart condition
ditali, i thimble-shaped pasta
dito, il (le dita) finger
divorziato/a divorced
doccia, la (le docce) shower
dodici twelve
dogana, la customs
dolce mild, sweet
dolce, il (i dolci) dessert
dolore, il (i dolori) hurt
domani tomorrow
domenica, la Sunday
donna, la (le donne) woman
donna d'affari, la (le donne)
    businesswoman
dopo after
dopobarba, la (le dopobarbe)
    aftershave
dopodomani day after tomorrow
doppio/a double
dorato/a golden (color)

dorso, il (i dorsi) back
dov'è where is
dove where
dritto straight ahead
drogheria, la (le drogherie) grocery
    store
due two
duecento two hundred
duomo, il (i duomi) cathedral
duro/a hard
e and
è you are, he is, she is
ecco here/there is/are!
economico/a cheap
edicola, l' *f* (le edicole) newstand
enoteca, l' *f* (le enoteche) liquor store
entrata, l' *f* (le entrate) admission
era it was
ero I was
errore, l' *m* (gli errori) mistake
espresso, l' *m* (gli espressi) espresso,
    strong black coffee
essere to be
esso/a it (subject)
est east
estate, l' *f* (le estati) summer
euro, l' *m* (gli euro) euro
fa you do, do you do?
faccia, la face
facciamo we do
faccio I do
fagiano, il (i fagiani) pheasant
fagioli alla toscana, i slow-cooked
    beans with salt, black pepper and
    olive oil
fagioli all'uccelletto, i beans cooked
    in tomatoes and black olives
fagioli in umido, i beans cooked in
    tomato sauce and spices
fagiolino, il (i fagiolini) green bean
fagiolo, il (i fagioli) dried bean
famiglia, la (le famiglie) family
fantastico/a fantastic, terrific
farcito/a stuffed
fare to do, to make
farfalle, la (le farfalli) butterfly-shaped
    pasta
farfallino, il (i farfallini) small, bow-
    shaped pasta

farmacia, la (le farmacie) drugstore
   (medicine), pharmacy
fava, la (le fave) broad beans
favata, la   bean and port stew
favore, il (i favori) favor
favore, per   please
fazzoletto di carta, il (i fazzoletti)
   facial tissue
febbraio   February
febbre, la   fever
fegato, il (i fegati) liver
fegato alla veneziana, il   liver fried
   with onions
felpa, la (le felpe) sweatshirt
fermo!   stop!
ferri, ai   grilled
ferroviaria, la stazione   train station
fetta, la (le fette) slice
fettuccine, le   ribbon-shaped pasta
fettuccine Alfredo, le   noodle
   ribbons with parmesan and cream
fico, il (i fichi) fig
figlia, la (le figlie) daughter
figlio, il (i figli) son
filetto, il (i filetti) fillet
filetto al pepe verde, il   steak in
   creamy sauce seasoned with green
   peppercorns
fine settimana, il   weekend
finestra, la (le finestre) window
finocchio, il   fennel
focaccia, la (le focacce) flatbread
fontana, la (le fontane) fountain
fonduta, la   fondue
forchetta, la (le forchette) fork
formaggi, quattro   (pizza) with four
   types of cheese
formaggio, il (i formaggi) cheese
forno, al   baked
forse   maybe
forte   loud, loudly
fortezza, la (le fortezze) fortress
fotocine, il negozio di   photo shop
fotografare   to photograph
fragola, la (le fragole) strawberry
Francia, la   France
francobollo, il (i francobolli) postage
   stamp
fratello, il (i fratelli) brother
freddo/a   cold

fresco/a   cool, fresh
frittata, la (le frittate) omelette
fritto/a   fried
fritto misto, il   fried mix of small fish
   and shellfish
frizzante   carbonated, fizzy
frullato di latte, il   milk-shake
frutta, la (le frutte) fruit
frutta secca, la   nuts, dried fruit
frutti di mare, i   seafood, shellfish
fumare   to smoke
fumare, il   smoking
fumatori   smokers
fumo, il   smoking, smoke
funghi porcini arrosti, i   porcini
   mushrooms roasted with garlic,
   parsley and chili peppers
fungho, il (i funghi) mushrooms
fuoco, il (i fuochi) fire
fuori   outside
fusillo, il (i fussili) pasta spiral
gabinetto, il (i gabinetti) bathroom
galletto amburghese, il   oven-
   roasted young chicken
gallo, il (i galli) rooster
gamba, la (le gambe) leg
gamberetto, il (i gamberetti) shrimps
gambere, il (i gamberi) prawns
gassato/a   carbonated
gatto, il (i gatti) cat
gelateria, la (le gelaterie) ice cream
   parlor
gelato, il (i gelati) ice cream
generoso/a   generous
genitore/trice, il/la (i genitori)
   parent
gennaio   January
Germania, la   Germany
ghetto, il (i ghetti) ghetto
ghiaccio, il   ice
ghiaccio, i cubetti di   ice cubes
giacca, la (le giacche) jacket
giallo/a   yellow
gianduia, la   cold chocolate pudding
giardino, il (i giardini) garden
gingerino   aperitif, ginger-flavored
ginocchio, il (le ginocchia) knee
giornale, il (i giornali) newspaper
giorno, il (i giorni) day
giovedì   Thursday

gita, la (le gite) trip
giù down
giugno June
gnocco, lo (gli gnocchi) small
dumpling from potato or semolina
gnoccho di patate, lo (gli gnocchi)
potato dumpling
gola, la throat
gomito, il (i gomiti) elbow
gonna, la (le gonne) skirt
gorgonzola, la a pungent blue cheese
grana padano, la a cheese similar to
Parmesan
granchio, il (i granchi) crab
grande big
graticola, alla barbequed
gratuito/a free, no cost
grazie thank you
grigio/a gray
griglia, alla grilled, broiled
grissino, il (i grissini) breadstick
guanto, il (i guanti) glove
guarda you look
guardando looking
guardare to look
guardaroba, il checkroom,
cloakroom
guardiamo we look
guardo I look
guida you drive
guidare to drive
guidiamo we drive
guido I drive
ha you have
ho I have
hot dog, l' *m* (gli hot dog) hot dog
idraulico/a, l'/l' *m/f* (gli idraulici/le
idrauliche) plumber
ieri yesterday
impanato/a breaded
imprenditrice, l' *f* businesswoman
in in
in bianco without tomato sauce, with
butter and Parmesan
includere to include
incrocio, l' *m* (gli incroci) crossroads
indivia, l' *f* endive
infermiere/a, l'/l' *m/f* (gli
infermieri/le infermiere) nurse

informazione, l' *f* (le informazioni)
information
ingegnere, l' *m* (gli ingegneri)
engineer
Inghilterra, l' *f* England
inglese English
ingorgo (del traffico), l' *m* (gli
ingorghi) traffic jam
ingresso, l' *m* (gli ingressi) admission,
admittance, entrance
ingresso gratuito, l' *m* free admission
insalata, l' *f* (le insalate) salad
insalata mista, l' *f* mixed salad
insegnante, l'/l' *m/f* (gli/le
insegnanti) teacher
inverno, l' *m* (gli inverni) winter
involtino, l' *m* (gli involtini) roulade,
rolled and stuffed slices of meat
io I
Italia, l' *f* Italy
Italiano Italian
I.V.A., l' *f* sales tax
jeans, i jeans
ketchup, il ketchup
la *f* it (direct object)
là there
lametta da barba, la (le lamette)
razor blade
lampada, la (le lampade) lamp
lampone, il (i lamponi) raspberry
lasagne, le *f* lasagna
lasagne con le verdure, le vegetable
lasagne
lattaiolo, il cinnamon custard
latte, il milk
lattuga, la (le lattughe) lettuce
lauro, il bay, laurel
leggero/a light (wine)
lei you
lentamente slow, slowly
lenticchia, la (le lenticchie) lentil
lepre, la (le lepri) hare
lesso/a boiled
lettera, la (le lettere) letter
letto, il (i letti) bed
letto matrimoniale, il (i letti) double
bed
libero/a available, vacant
libreria, la (le librerie) bookstore
libro, il (i libri) book

limonata, la lemonade
limone, il (i limoni) lemon
lingua, la (le lingue) tongue
linguine, le f thick spaghetti
liquore, il (i liquori) liqueur
lista dei vini, la (le liste) wine list
litro, il (i litri) liter
L'IVA f sales tax
lo m it (direct object)
locale, il (i locali) local
locanda, la (le locande) inn, simple
    restaurant with local dishces
lombata, la (le lombate) loin steak
lontano/a far away
luce, la (le luci) light
luglio July
lumaca, la (le lumache) snail
lumache alle milanese, le snails with
    sauce (anchovy, fennel, wine)
lunedì Monday
lunette, le filled half-moon pasta
lungo/a long
lui he
ma but
maccheroni, i macaroni
macchiato/a with milk
macchina fotografica, la (le
    macchine) camera
madre, la (le madri) mother
magazzino, il grande department
    store
maggio May
maggiorana, la marjoram
maglione, il (i maglioni) sweater,
    pullover
maiale, il pork
maionese, la mayonnaise
mais, il corn
mal di testa, il headache
mancia, la (le mance) tip (for service)
mandarino, il (i mandarini) tangerine
mandorla, la (le mandorle) almond
mangia you eat
mangiamo we eat
mangiare to eat
mangio I eat
mano, la (le mani) hand
manovale, il (i manovali) laborer
manzo, il beef
mappa, la (le mappe) map

mare, il (i mari) sea
margherita, la (pizza) with tomato,
    cheese and basil
marinara, alla sauce of tomatoes,
    olives, garlic, clams and mussels
marinato/a marinated
marito, il (i mariti) husband
marmellata, la (le marmellate) jam
marrone brown
martedì Tuesday
Martini vermouth, sweet or dry
marzo March
mascarpone, il a cream cheese
mattina, la (le mattine) morning
meccanico/a, il/la (i meccanici/le
    meccaniche) mechanic
medaglione, il (i medaglioni) round
    fillet, medaillon
medicina, la medicine
medicinale, il (i medicinali)
    medication
medico/a, il/la (i medici/le mediche)
    doctor
medio/a middle
meglio better
mela, la (le mele) apple
melanzana, la (le melanzane)
    eggplant
melone, il (i meloni) (musk)melon
meno fewer, less, minus
menta, la (le mente) mint
menù, il menu
menù a prezzo fisso, il set-priced
    menu
menù turistico, il tourist menu
mercato, il (i mercati) market
mercoledì Wednesday
merluzzo, il (i merluzzi) cod
mese, il (i mesi) month
metro, il subway
metropolitana, la subway
mezzo/a half, middle
mezzogiorno, il noon
mezzanotte, la midnight
miele, il honey
milanese, alla with marrow, white
    wine, saffron, Parmesan
milione, il (i milioni) million
mille (mila) thousand

Millefiore liqueur flavored with herbs and alpine flowers
minestra, la soup
minestrone, il thick vegetable and pasta soup
minuto, il (i minuti) minute
mio/a my
mirtillo, il (i mirtilli) blueberries
misto/a mixed
moglie, la wife
molle soft
molto/a a lot, much, a great deal
momento, il (i momenti) moment
montone, il mutton
mora, la (le more) blackberry
mortadella, la Bologna sausage
mostarda, la mustard
motocicletta, la (le motociclette) motorcycle
mozzarella, la a moist, mild, rubbery white cheese
muro, il (i muri) wall
museo, il (i musei) museum
musicista, il/la (i musicisti/le musiciste) musician
mutande, le underpants
napoletana, la (pizza) with anchovies, ham, tomatoes, capers, cheese and oregano
naso, il nose
Natale, il Christmas
naturale non-carbonated
nebbioso/a foggy
negozio, il (i negozi) shop, store
nero/a black
nevica it's snowing
nipote (di nonni), il/la (i nipoti/le nipoti) grandson/granddaughter
nipote (di zii), il/la (i nipoti/le nipoti) nephew/niece
no no
nocciola, la (le nocciole) hazelnut
noce, il (i noci) walnut
noce di cocco, la (le noci) coconut
noce moscata, la (le noci) nutmeg
nocepesca, la (le nocepesche) nectarine
nodino, il (i nodini) veal chops
noi we
noleggiare to rent

nome, il (i nomi) name
non not
nonna, la grandmother
nonni, i grandparents
nonno, il grandfather
non potabile not safe to drink
nord north
Norma, alla with spices and tomato sauce
nostro/a our
notte, la (le notti) night
notte, questa tonight
novanta ninety
nove nine
novecento nine hundred
novembre November
nubile, la single woman
numero, il (i numeri) number
nuvoloso/a cloudy
o or
oca, l' *f* (le oche) goose
occhiali, gli eyeglasses
occhiali da sole, gli sunglasses
occhio, l' *m* (gli occhi) eye
occupato/a occupied, taken
odori, gli herbs
offerta, l' *f* (le offerte) offer
oggi today
olio, l' *m* (gli oli) oil
olio d'oliva, l' *m* olive oil
olio solare, l' *m* suntan oil
oliva, l' *f* (le olive) olive
ombrello, l' *m* (gli ombrelli) umbrella
ombrellone, l' *m* (gli ombrelloni) sun umbrella
ora, l' *f* (le ore) hour
orario di apertura, l' *m* hours of business
ordinare to place an order
orecchiette, le ear-shaped pasta
orecchio, l' *m* (le orecchie) ear
origano, l' *m* oregano
orologio, l' *m* (gli orologi) clock
orologio da polso, l' *m* wristwatch
orrendo/a horrendous, horrble
ospedale, l' *m* (gli ospedali) hospital
osteria, l' *f* (le osterie) inn (wine and simple food)
ostrica, l' *f* (le ostriche) oyster
ottanta eighty

otto eight
ottobre October
ottocento eight hundred
ovest west
padre, il (i padri) father
pagare to pay
palazzo, il (i palazzi) palace
pan di Spagna, il honey-rum sponge cake
pancetta, la bacon
pandoro, il sponge cake topped with powdered vanilla, eaten at Christmas
pane, il bread
pane tostato, il toast
panetteria, la (le panetterie) bakery
panettone, il spiced brioche, eaten at Christmas
panino, il (i panini) roll
panino imbottito, il sandwich, filled roll
paninoteca, la (le paninoteche) sandwich shop
panna montata, la whipped cream
pantaloni, i pants
pappardella, la (le pappardelle) fat ribbon noodle
parcheggio, il (i parcheggi) parking lot
parchimetro, il (i parchimetri) parking meter
parco, il (i parchi) park
parla you speak
parlare to speak
parlo I speak
parmigiana, alla made or covered with Parmesan cheese
parmigiano, il very hard, dry, sharp cheese
parrucchiere, il (i parrucchieri) hairdresser, barber
parte, la (le parti) part
partenza, la (le partenze) departure
passaporto, il (i passaporti) passport
passato di verdura, il vegetable purèe
pasta, la pasta, dough, pastry, cake
pastasciutta, la pasta
pasticca per la tosse, la (le pasticche) cough drop

pasticceria, la pastry shop
pasticcino, il (i pasticcino) pastries, petit four
pastina, la small pasta shapes used in soup
pastore, il (i pastori) minister
patata, la (le patate) potato
patate fritte, le French fries
patatine fritte, le French fries
patente di guida, la (le patenti) driver's license
pavese, la zuppa alla clear soup with poached egg, croutons, cheese
pavimento, il floor (of room)
pecorino, il variety of cheeses made from sheep's milk
pedaggio, il (i pedaggi) toll
pelle, la skin
penicillina, la penicillin
penna, la (le penne) pen, feather, pasta quill
pensione, la (le pensioni) boarding house, pension
pensione, in retired
pepe, il pepper
peperonata, la stewed peppers, tomatoes, onions
peperone, il (i peperoni) peppers, capsicum
peperoni ripieni, i stuffed peppers
per for, to
pera, la (le pere) pear
perché why
per favore please
pericolo, il (i pericoli) danger
pericolo di morte, il danger to life
permesso? May I get past?
pernice, la (le pernici) partridge
persona, la (le persone) person
per via aerea by airmail
pesca, la (le pesche) peach
pescatora, alla with tomatoes and seafood
pesce, il (i pesci) fish
pesce persico, il perch
pesce spada, il swordfish
petto, il chest
piace, mi it is pleasing to me (=I like it)
piacere, il (i piaceri) pleasure, favor

piacciono, mi   they are pleasing to
me (=I like them)
piacere, per   please
piatto, il (i piatti) dish, plate, course,
meal
piatto del giorno, il   specialty of the
day
piatto di carne, il (i piatti) meat dish
piazza, la (le piazze) square
piazza principale, la   main square,
town square
piccante   sharp (flavor), spicy
piccata alla marsala, la   veal in
marsala sauce
piccione, il (i piccioni) pigeon
piccolo/a   small, little
piede, il (i piedi) foot
pieno/a   full-bodied (wine)
pila, la (le pile) battery
pinolo, il (i pinoli) pine nut
piove   it's raining
piselli, i   peas
più   more
pizza, la (le pizze) pizza
pneumatico, lo (gli pneumatici) tire
po' (di), un   a little (of)
poco, un   a little
poi   then
polenta., la   cornmeal mush
polenta alla piemontese, la
cornmeal mush layered with meat
polenta e coniglio, la   cornmeal
mush and rabbit stew
polipo, il (i polipi) octopus
polizia, la   police
pollame, il   poultry, fowl
pollo, il (i polli) chicken
pollo all'abruzzese, il   chicken with
sweet peppers
pollo alla diavola, il   spicy grilled
chicken
pollo alla romana, il   chicken, tomato
sauce, sweet peppers
pollo novello, il   spring chicken
polpetta di carne, la (le polpette)
meatball
polpettina, la (le polpettine) tiny
meatball
polpettone, il   meatloaf
polpo, il (i polpi) octopus

pomeriggio, il (i pomeriggi)
afternoon
pommarola, la   tomato, garlic, basil
sauce
pompelmo, il (i pompelmi)
grapefruit
pomodoro, il (i pomodori) tomato
pompiere, il (i pompieri) fireman
ponte, il (i ponti) bridge
porchetta, la   roast suckling pig
porcini, i   type of mushroom
porro, il (i porri) leek
portacenere, il (i portaceneri) ashtray
porta, la (le porte) door
porto, il (i porti) port
possiamo   we can, we are able to, we
may
posso   I can, I am able to, I may
posta, la   mail
postale, l'ufficio   post office
potabile   drinkable, safe to drink
potere   to be able to, can, may
potrebbe   you could, you might be
able to
potrei   I could, I might be able to
pranzo, il (i pranzi) lunch
prego   you're welcome
prenda!   take!
prendere   to take
prendo   I take
prenotazione, la (le prenotazioni)
reservation
pressione, la   pressure
pressione alta, la   high bood pressure
pressione del sangue, la   blood
pressure
presto   early, soon
prete, il (i preti) priest
prezzemolo, il   parsley
prezzo, il (i prezzi) price
prezzo fisso, il **menù a**   set-priced
menu
prima di   before
primavera, la (le primavere) spring
primo piatto, il   first course
professore/essa, il/la (i professori/le
professoresse) professor
profumeria, la   perfumery
profumo, il (profumi) perfume

programmatore/trice di computer, il/la (i programmatori/le programmatrici) computer programmer

pronto/a ready, quick

prosciutto, il ham

prosciutto cotto, il ham, cooked or boiled

prosciutto crudo, il cured ham

provolone, il firm, often smoked cheese

prugna, la (le prugne) plum

prugna secca, la prune

pulito/a clean

pullman, il (i pullman) town-to-town bus; coach

puntino/a medium (meat)

può you are able to

purè, in creamed

puttanesca, alla sauce of anchovies, capers, black olives and tomatoes

quaglia, la (le quaglie) quail

qualche a few

qualcosa something

quale what

quando when

quanto how much, how long

quante how many (fem.)

quanti how many

quaranta forty

quarto, il (i quarti) quarter

quasi crudo/a very rare (meat)

quattordici fourteen

quattro four

quattrocento four hundred

quattro formaggi four types of cheese (pizza)

quattro stagioni vegetables, cheese, ham, bacon (pizza)

quello/a that (thing)

questa notte tonight

questo/a this, these

qui here

quindici fifteen

radicchio, il red lettuce

raffreddore, il cold

ragazza, la (le ragazze) girl, young woman, girlfriend

ragazzo, il (i ragazzi) boy, young man, boyfriend

ragioniere/a, il/la (i/le ragionieri/e) accountant

ragù, al meat sauce for pasta

rappresentante di commercio, il/la (i/le rappresentanti) sales representative

ravanello, il (i ravanelli) radish

ravioli alla piemontese, i ravioli filled with beef and vegetables

regali, il negozio di gift shop

reggiseno, il (i reggiseni) bra

regolare regular, medium

ribes, il red currant

ribes nero, il black currant

ricetta, la (le ricette) prescription

ricevuta, la (le ricevute) receipt

ricotta, la a white, unripened cheese similar to cottage cheese

rigatoni, i stubby pasta tubes

ripetere to repeat

ripieno/a stuffed

riscaldamento, il heating

risi e bisi, i rice with beans and bacon

riso, il rice

ristorante, il (i ristoranti) restaurant

ritardo, il (i ritardi) delay

ritorno, il (i ritorni) return trip, return

rivista, la (le riviste) magazine

rognone, il (i rognoni) kidney

rollino, il (i rollini) roll of film

rosa pink

rosato, il rosé (wine)

rosatello, il rosé (wine)

rosbif, il roast beef

rosmarino, il rosemary

rosso/a red

rotto/a broken

rullino, il (i rullini) roll of film

rumoroso/a noisy

ruota, la (le ruote) wheel

rustica, alla with garlic, anchovies, oregano

sabato Saturday

salame, il salami

saldi sales

sale, il salt

salmone, il salmon

salsa, la (le salse) sauce

salsiccia, la (le salsicce) sausage

saltato/a sautéed

saltimbocca, il   rolled veal and ham
   with sage, served in a wine sauce
salumi, i   cured pork products, cold
   cuts
salvia, la   sage
sambuca, la   anise-flavored liqueur
sandalo, il   (i sandali)   sandal
sangue, il   blood
sangue, al   rare (meat)
saponetta, la   (le saponette)   bar of
   soap
sardina, la   (le sardine)   sardine
scalogno, lo   (gli scalogni)   shallot
scaloppina, la   (le scaloppine)   veal
   cutlet
scaloppina alla Valdostana, la   veal
   cutlet filled with ham and cheese
scampo, lo   (gli scampi)   prawn
scarpa, la   (le scarpe)   shoe
scelta, la   (le scelte)   choice, selection
scendere   to go down, descend
schiena, la   back
sciarpa, la   (le sciarpe)   scarf
scienziato/a, lo/la   (gli scienziati/le
   scienziate)   scientist
sciroppo per la tosse, lo   cough
   syrup
scontrino, lo   (gli scontrini)   receipt
   (when prepaying for item, e.g., at a
   bar)
scrivere   to write
scuro/a   dark
scusi, (mi)   Excuse me, I apologize
secco/a   dry (wine)
secondo, il   (i secondi)   second
secondo piatto, il   main (second)
   course
sedano, il   (i sedani)   celery
sedia, la   (le sedie)   chair
sedici   sixteen
segretario/a, il/la   (i segretari/le
   segretarie)   secretary
sei   six
seicento   six hundred
semifreddo   chilled dessert made with
   ice cream
semplice   simple
sempre   always
senape, la   mustard
senza   without

separatamente   separately
separato/a   separated
sera, la   (le sere)   evening
servizio, il   (i servizi)   service
sessanta   sixty
settanta   seventy
sette   seven
settecento   seven hundred
settembre   September
settimana, la   (le settimane)   week
settimana, il fine   weekend
sgombro, lo   mackerel
shampoo, lo   shampoo
shorts, gli   shorts
sì   yes
siamo   we are
siciliana   (pizza) with capers, black
   olives and cheese
sigaretta, la   (le sigarette)   cigarette
signora, la   (le signore)   lady
signore, il   (i signori)   gentleman
signorina, la   (le signorine)   miss,
   young woman
Silvestro   herb/nut liqueur
singolo/a   single
sinistra   left
snack-bar, lo   snack bar
sodo/a   hard, firm
soffitto, il   (i soffitti)   ceiling
sogliola, la   sole
sogliole alla mugnaia, le   sole
   cooked in butter and served with
   parsley and lemon
soldi, i   money
solo/a   only
solubile   instant (coffee)
sono   I am
sopra   on
sorella, la   (le sorelle)   sister
sottaceti, (i)   pickled (vegetables)
sotto   under
sottolio   in oil
spaghetti, gli   spaghetti
spaghetti all'amatriciana, gli
   spaghetti with sauce of tomato,
   bacon and Pecorino cheese
Spagna, la   Spain
spalla, la   (le spalle)   shoulder
specialità, la   speciality
speziato/a   spicy

spezie, le spices
spezzatino, lo stew
spiedino, lo kebab
spiedo, allo broiled, roasted on spit
spina, alla draft (beer)
spinaci, gli spinach
spingere to press, to push
sporco/a dirty
sposato/a married
spumante, lo (gli spumanti) sparkling
  (wine)
spuntino, lo (gli spuntini) snack
stadio, lo (gli stadi) stadium
stagioni, quattro (pizza) with
  various vegetables, cheese, ham and
  bacon
stasera tonight
Stati Uniti, gli the United States
stazione di servizio, la (le stazioni)
  gas station
stazione ferroviaria, la train station
stecca di cioccolato, la (le stecche)
  chocolate bar
stelline, le little pasta stars
stitichezza, la constipation
stoccafisso, lo dried cod
stomaco, lo stomach
stomaco, il mal di stomach ache
storico/a historical
storione, lo sturgeon
stracciatella, la clear soup of egg,
  cheese and semolina; vanilla ice
  cream with chocolate chips
straniero/a foreign
strapazzate scrambled (eggs)
Strega sweet herb liqueur
studente/essa, lo/la (gli studenti/le
  studentesse) student
stufato/a braised
stufato, lo (gli stufati) stew
su on, up
subito right away, immediately
succo, il (i succhi) juice
succo di frutta, il fruit juice
succo di mela, il apple juice
sud south
sugo, il (i sughi) sauce
suora, la (le suore) nun
su ordinazione made to order

supermercato, il (i supermercati)
  supermarket
supplemento/a extra,
  supplementary
supplì, i fried rice croquettes
susina, la (le susine) plum
Svizzera, la Switzerland
tabaccheria, la (le tabaccherie)
  tobacconist's shop
tacchino, il (i tacchini) turkey
tagliatelle, le pasta ribbons, fettucine
tagliato/a a cubetti diced
tardi late
tartufi di cioccolata, i chocolate
  truffles
tartufo, il (i tartufi) truffle
tassì, il (i tassì) taxi
taverna, la (le taverne) tavern;
  modest, simple restaurant
tavola, la (le tavole) table
tavola calda, la warm snack bar
tavola fredda, la cold snack bar
taxi, il (i taxi) taxi
tè, il tea
tè freddo, il iced tea
telefonino, il (i telefonini) cell phone
telefono, il (i telefoni) telephone
tempo, il time, weather
terribile terrible
testa, la head
timo, il thyme
tiramisù, il sponge cake soaked in
  coffee, topped with mascarpone,
  eggs, chocolate/coffee powders
tirare to pull
tisana, la (le tisane) herb tea
toccare to touch
toccare!, non don't touch!
toeletta, la (le toelette) restroom,
  toilet, WC
toilette, la restroom, toilet, WC
tonno, il tuna
tonsilla, la (le tonsille) tonsil
torace, il chest
tordo, il (i tordi) thrush (bird)
torrone, il nougat
torta, la (le torte) cake, pie
torta manfreda, la liver pate with
  Parmesan and Marsala

torta Margherita, la cake with
   meringue, fruit, whipped cream
tortellini, i small filled dough rings
   with sauce or in soup
tortino, il (i tortini) savory pie
tostato/a toasted
tovagliolo, il (i tovaglioli) napkin
tra between, among
traghetto, il (i traghetti) ferry
tram, il (i tram) streetcar, tram
tranquillo/a quiet
trattoria, la (le trattorie) usually
   inexpensive restaurant serving
   simple food
tre three
trecento three hundred
tredici thirteen
treno, il (i treni) train
trenta thirty
triglia, la (le triglie) mullet
trippa, la tripe
troppo too
trota, la (le trote) trout
T-shirt, la T-shirt
turista, il/la (i turisti/le turiste) tourist
turistico/a tourist (adj.)
tutto all, the whole
uccello, l' *m* (gli uccelli) bird
ufficio, l' *m* (gli uffici) office
umido, in stewed
undici eleven
unico/a combined
unico, a senso one-way traffic
uno one
uomo, l' *m* (gli uomini) man
uomo d'affari, l' *m* (gli uomini)
   businessman
uova alla romana, le omelet with
   beans, onions, herbs
uovo, l' *m* (le uova) egg
uscita, l' *f* (le uscite) exit
uva, l' *f* (le uva) grape
uva passa, l' *f* (l'uva passa) raisin
uva spina, l' *f* (l'uva spina)
   gooseberry
va you go
vada! go!
vado I go
vai via! go away!
valigia, la (le valige) bag, suitcase

valuta, la currency
vaniglia, la vanilla
vapore, al steamed
vaporetto, il (i vaporetti) waterbus
vecchio/a old
vedere to see
vedovo/a widowed
venerdì Friday
venire to come
venti twenty
vento, tira it's windy
ventoso/a windy
verde green; creamed green
   vegetables
verdura, la vegetables
verdura mista, la mixed vegetables
verdure di stagione, le vegetables in
   season
vermicelli, i very thin spaghetti
verza, la (le verze) green cabbage
vestito, il (i vestiti) dress
via aerea air mail
viaggio, il (i viaggi) trip
vicino nearby
vietato/a forbidden, prohibited
vino, il (i vini) wine
vino della casa, il house wine
vino, la lista dei wine list
viola purple
viso, il (i visi) face
vitello, il veal
vitello alla bolognese, il veal cutlet
   with Parma ham and cheese
volo, il (i voli) flight
vongola, la (le vongole) clams
vongole, alle sauce of clams, garlic,
   pepper, olive oil, parsley, possibly
   tomatoes
vongole, la zuppa di clam, white-
   wine soup
vorrei I would like
vorremmo we would like
WC, il bathroom
würstel, il hot dogs, wieners
zabaglione, lo egg yolks, sugar,
   Marsala wine
zafferano, lo saffron
zenzero, lo ginger
zero, lo zero
zia, la (le zie) aunt

zio, lo (gli zii) uncle
ziti, i medium-sized pasta tubes
zucca, la pumpkin, gourd
zucchero, lo sugar
zucchino, lo (gli zucchini) zucchini
zucchini ripieni, gli stuffed zucchini
zuppa, la (le zuppe) soup
zuppa del giorno, la soup of the day

zuppa inglese, la rum-soaked
sponge cake filled with cream and
chocolate or candied fruit

English-Italian Dictionary

How to use this dictionary

The purpose of this dictionary is to help you find and pronounce the Italian words you will most likely need to communicate as a visitor in Italy.

English words are listed in bold. Most Italian verbs are listed in infinitive form; you will need to change them to get the *io* and *Lei* forms. Some irregular verb forms are included, however. Most nouns are listed in singular; if you need plural forms, look up the Italian word in the Italian-English dictionary.

able to, I am　posso *(pohs-soh)*

able to, to be　potere *(poh-tay-ray)*

able to, we are　possiamo *(pohs-syah-moh)*

able to, you are　può *(pwoh)*

accountant　ragioniere/a, il/la *(rah-joh-nyeh-ray/-rah)*

admission　entrata, l' *f (ayn-trah-tah)*; ingresso, l' *m (een-grehs-soh)*

admission, free　ingresso gratuito, l' *m (een-grehs-soh grah-too-ee-toh)*

admittance　ingresso, l' *m (een-grehs-soh)*

admittance ticket　biglietto, il *(beel-lyayt-toh)*

adult　adulto/a, l'/l' *m/f (ah-dool-toh/-tah)*

after　dopo *(doh-poh)*

afternoon　pomeriggio, il *(poh-may-reed-joh)*

afternoon, in the　del pomeriggio *(dayl poh-may-reed-joh)*

aftershave　dopobarba, il *(doh-poh-bahr-bah)*

against　contro *(kohn-troh)*

ahead　avanti *(ah-vahn-tee)*

air conditioning　aria condizionata, l' *f (ahr-yah kohn-deet-tsyoh-nah-tah)*

airmail, by　per via aerea *(payr vee-ah ah-eh-ray-ah)*

airplane　aeroplano, l' *m (ah-ay-roh-plah-noh)*

airport　aeroporto, l' *m (ah-ay-roh-pohr-toh)*

all, that's　È tutto *(ay toot-toh)*

allergic　allergico/a *(ahl-lehr-jee- koh/-kah)*

alphabet　alfabeto, l' *m (ahl-fah-bay-toh)*

also　anche *(ahn-kay)*

always　sempre *(sehm-pray)*

am, I　sono *(soh-noh)*

ambulance　ambulanza, l' *f (ahm-boo-lahn-tsah)*

America　America, l' *f (ah-may-ree-kah)*

anchovies　acciughe, le *(aht-choo-gay)*

and　e *(ay)*

antacid　antiacido, l' *m (ahn-tyah-chee- doh)*

antihistamine　antistaminico, l' *m (ahn-tees-tah-mee-nee-koh)*

appetite　appetito, l' *m (ahp-pay-tee-toh)*

appetizer　antipasto, l' *m (ahn-tee-pah-stoh)*

apple　mela, la *(may-lah)*

apple juice　succo di mela, il *(sook-koh dee-may-lah)*

April　aprile *(ah-pree-lay)*

architect　architetto, l' *m (ahr-kee-tayt-toh)*

are, we　siamo *(syah-moh)*

are, you　è *(eh)*

arm　braccio, il *(braht-choh)*

arrival　arrivo, l' *m (ahr-ree-voh)*

artichoke　carciofo, il *(kahr-choh-foh)*

artist　artista, l'/l' *m/f (ahr-tees-tah)*

ashtray　portacenere, il *(pohr-tah-chay-nay-ray)*

asparagus asparagi, gli *(ahs-pah-rah-jee)*
aspirin aspirina, l' *f (ahs-pee-ree-nah)*
ATM bancomat, il *(bahn-koh-maht)*
ATM card carta bancomat, la *(kahr-tah bahn-koh-maht)*
attention! attenzione! *(aht-tayn-tsyoh-nay)*
August agosto *(ah-goh-stoh)*
aunt zia, la *(tsee-ah)*
Austria Austria, l' *f (ow-stree-ah)*
automatic transmission cambio automatico, il *(kahm-byoh ow-toh-mah-tee-koh)*
autumn autunno, l' *m (aw-toon-noh)*
available libero/a *(lee-bay-roh/-rah)*
away, far lontano/a *(lohn-tah-noh/-nah)*
baby bambino/a, il/la *(bahm-bee-noh/-nah)*
back dorso, il *(dohr-soh)*; schiena, la *(skyeh-nah)*
bacon pancetta, la *(pahn-chay-tah*
bad brutto/a *(broot-toh/-tah)*; cattivo/a *(kaht-tee-voh/-vah)*
bag (suitcase) valigia, la *(vah-leej-jah)*
bakery panetteria, la *(pah-nayt-tay-ree-ah)*
ballpoint pen penna a sfera, la *(payn-nah a sfeh-rah)*
banana banana, la *(bah-nah-nah)*
B and B pensione, la *(payn-syoh-nay)*
bank banca, la *(bahn-kah)*
barber barbiere, il *(bahr-byeh-ray)*
bar bar, il *(bahr)*
bath bagno, il *(bahn-nyoh)*
bathing suit costume da bagno, il *(kohs-too-may dah bahn-nyoh)*
bathing trunks costume da bagno, il *(kohs-too-may dah bahn-nyoh)*
bathroom toeletta, la *(toh-ay-leht-tah)*; gabinetto, il *(gah-bee-nayt-toh)*, il *(vee-chee)*; bagno, il *(bahn-nyoh)*
battery pila, la *(pee-lah)*; (for car) batteria, la *(baht-tay-ree-ah)*
be, to essere *(ehs-say-ray)*
beans, dried fagioli, i *(fahd-joh-lee)*
beans, green fagiolini *(fahd-joh-lee-nee)*
beef manzo, il *(mahn-dzoh)*
beef broth brodo di manzo, il *(broh-doh dee mahn-dzoh)*
beer birra, la *(beer-rah)*
before prima di *(pree-mah dee)*
begin, to cominciare *(koh-meen-chah-ray)*

beige beige *(bayzh)*
bench banco, il *(bahn-koh)*
better meglio *(mehl-lyoh)*
between tra *(trah)*
bicycle bicicletta, la *(bee-chee-klayt-tah)*
big grande *(grahn-day)*
bike bicicletta, la *(bee-chee-klayt-tah)*
bird uccello, l' *m (oot-chehl-loh)*
birthday compleanno, il *(kohm-play-ahn-noh)*
bitter amaro/a *(ah-mah-roh/-rah)*
black nero/a *(nay-roh/-rah)*
blood pressure pressione del sangue, la *(prays-syoh-nay dayl sahn-gway)*
blouse camicetta, la *(kah-mee-chayt-tah)*
blue blu *(bloo)*
book libro, il *(lee-broh)*
bookstore libreria, la *(lee-bray-ree-ah)*
bottle bottiglia, la *(boht-teel-lyah)*
boy ragazzo, il *(rah-gaht-tsoh)*
boyfriend ragazzo, il *(rah-gaht-tsoh)*
bra reggiseno, il *(rayj-jee-say-noh)*
bread pane, il *(pah-nay)*
breakfast colazione, la *(koh-laht-tsyoh-nay)*
bridge ponte, il *(pohn-tay)*
broken rotto/a *(roht-toh/-tah)*
broth brodo, il *(broh-doh)*
brother fratello, il *(frah-tehl-loh)*
brown marrone *(mahr-roh-nay)*
burger hamburger, l' *(ahm-boor-gayr)*
bus (within city) autobus, l' *m (ow-toh-boos)*; (town-to-town) pullman, il *(pool-mahn)*
businessman uomo d'affari, l' *m (woh-moh dahf-fah-ray)*
businesswoman imprenditrice, l' *f (eem-prayn-dee-tree-chay)*; donna d'affari, la *(dohn-nah dahf-fah-ray)*
but ma *(mah)*
butter burro, il *(boor-roh)*
'bye Ciao! *(chow)*
cab taxi, il *(tahk-see)*; tassì, il *(tahs-see)*
cabbage cavolo, il *(kah-voh-loh)*
café bar, il *(bahr)*
cake torta, la *(tohr-tah)*
call! Chiami! *(kyah-mee)*
call, to chiamare *(kyah-mah-ray)*
camera macchina fotografica, la *(mah-kee-nah foh-toh-grah-fee-kah)*

camera shop negozio di fotocine, il *(nay-goht-tsyoh dee foh-toh-chee-nay)*
can (=be able to) potere *(poh-tay-ray)*
can, I posso *(poh-soh)*
can, we possiamo *(pohs-syah-moh)*
can you? può? *(pwoh?)*
can, you può *(pwoh)*
Canada Canada, il *(kah-nah-dah)*
candy caramella, la *(kah-rah-mehl-lah)*
cappuccino cappuccino, il *(kahp-poot-chee-noh)*
car auto, l' *m* *(ow-toh)*
carafe caraffa, la *(kah-rahf-fah)*
carbonated gassato/a *(gahs-sah-toh/-tah)*; frizzante *(freed-zahn-tay)*
careful! attento! *(aht-tahn-toh)*; attenzione! *(aht-tayn-tsyoh-nay)*
carpenter carpentiere, il *(kahr-payn-tyeh-ray)*
carrot carota, la *(kah-roh-tah)*
cash (pay with) in contanti *(een kohn-tahn-tee)*
cash card carta bancomat, la *(kahr-tah bahn-koh-maht)*
cash machine bancomat, il *(bahn-koh-maht)*
cash register cassa, la *(kahs-sah)*
castle castello, il *(kahs-tehl-loh)*
cat gatto, il *(gaht-toh)*
cathedral duomo, il *(dwoh-moh)*; cattedrale, la *(kaht-tay-drah-lay)*
cauliflower cavolfiore, il *(kah-vohl-fyoh-ray)*
ceiling soffitto, il *(sohf-feet-toh)*
center of town centro, il *(chehn-troh)*
chair sedia, la *(sehd-yah)*
cheap economico/a *(ay-koh-noh-mee-koh/-kah)*
cheaper più economico/a *(pyoo ay-koh-noh-mee-koh/-kah)*
check, please! Il conto, per piacere! *(eel kohn-toh, payr pyah-chay-ray)*
checkroom guardaroba, la *(gwahr-dah-roh-bah)*
cheese formaggio, il *(fohr-mahd-joh)*
cherry ciliegia, la *(chee-lyehd-jah)*
chest torace, il *(toh-rah-chay)*; petto, il *(peht-toh)*
chewing gum gomma da masticare, la *(gohm-mah dah mahs-tee-kah-ray)*
chicken pollo, il *(pohl-loh)*
chicken broth brodo di pollo, il *(broh-doh dee pohl-loh)*

child bambino/a, il/la *(bahm-bee-noh/-nah)*
chocolate cioccolato, il *(chohk-koh-lah-toh)*
Christmas Natale, il *(nah-tah-lay)*
church chiesa, la *(kyay-zah)*
cigarettes sigarette, le *(see-gah-rayt-tay)*
city città, la *(cheet-tah)*
clean pulito/a *(poo-lee-toh/-tah)*
clear chiaro/a *(kyah-roh/-rah)*
cloakroom guardaroba, la *(gwahr-dah-roh-bah)*
clock orologio, l' *m* *(oh-roh-loh-joh)*
closed (to be) chiuso/a *(kyoo-soh/-sah)*
clothes abbigliamento, l' *m* *(ahb-beel-lyah-mayn-toh)*
cloudy nuvoloso/a *(noo-voh-loh-soh/-sah)*
coach (=bus) pullman, il *(pool-mahn)*
coat cappotto, il *(kahp-poht-toh)*
coffee caffè, il *(kahf-feh)*
cold freddo/a *(frayd-doh/-dah)*
cold (illness) raffreddore, il *(rahf-frayd-doh-ray)*
cold cuts salumi, i *(sah-loo-mee)*; affettato, l' *m* *(ahf-fayt-tah-toh)*
color colore, il *(koh-loh-ray)*
combined (as in the bill) unico/a *(oo-nee-koh/-kah)*
come, to venire *(vay-nee-ray)*
computer programmer programmatore/trice di computer, il/la *(proh-grahm-mah-toh-ray/-tree-chay dee kum-pyoo-tur)*
cone cornetto, il *(kohr-nayt-toh)*
constipation stitichezza, la *(stee-tee-kayt-tsah)*
cooked cotto/a *(koht-toh/-tah)*
cookie biscotto, il *(bees-koht-toh)*
cool fresco/a *(fray-skoh/-skah)*
corn mais, il *(mah-ees)*
cost, to costare *(koh-stah-ray)*
cough drop pasticca per la tosse, la *(pahs-teek-kah payr lah tohs-say)*
cough syrup sciroppo per la tosse, lo *(shee-rohp-poh payr lah tohs-say)*
could, I potrei *(poh-treh-ee)*
could, you potrebbe *(poh-trehb-bee)*
course (food) piatto, il *(pyah-toh)*
cousin cugino/a, il/la *(koo-jee-noh/-nah)*
cover charge (il prezzo del) coperto *(koh-pehr-toh)*
covering copertura, la *(koh-payr-too-rah)*
crab granchio, il *(grahnk-yoh)*

cream crema, la *(kreh-mah)*

credit card carta di credito, la *(kahr-tah dee kray-dee-toh)*

croissant cornetto, il *(kohr-nayt-toh)*

crossroads incrocio, l' *m (een-kroht-choh)*

cucumber cetriolo, il *(chay-tree-oh-loh)*

currency valuta, la *(vah-loo-tah)*

currency exchange office cambio, il *(kahm-byoh)*; ufficio di cambio, l' *m (oof-fee-choh dee kahm-byoh)*

customs dogana, la *(doh-gah-nah)*

danger! pericolo!, il *(pay-ree-koh-loh)*

danger of death pericolo di morte, il *(pay-ree-koh-loh dee mohr-tay)*

dark scuro/a *(skoo-roh/-rah)*

date data, la *(dah-tah)*

daughter figlia, la *(feel-lyah)*

day giorno, il *(johr-noh)*

decaf decaffeinato/a *(day-kahf-fay-ee-nah-toh/-tah)*

deceased deceduto/a *(day-chay-doo-toh/-tah)*

December dicembre *(dee-chehm-bray)*

decongestant decongestionante, il *(day-kohn-jay-styoh-nahn-tay)*

delay ritardo, il *(ree-tahr-doh)*

deodorant deodorante, il *(day-oh-doh-rahn-tay)*

department store grande magazzino, il *(grahn-day mah-gaht-tsee-noh)*

departure partenza, la *(pahr-tehnt-sah)*

dessert dolce, il *(dohl-chay)*

diabetic diabetico/a *(dee-ah-beh-tee-koh/-kah)*

diarrhea diarrea, la *(dee-ahr-reh-ah)*

diet dietetico/a *(dee-ay-teh-tee-koh/-kah)*

dirty sporco/a *(spohr-koh/-kah)*

dish (kind of food) piatto, il *(pyah-toh)*

divorced divorziato/a *(dee-vohr-tsyah-toh/-tah)*

do, to fare *(fah-ray)*

do, I faccio *(faht-choh))*

do, we facciamo *(faht-chah-moh)*

do, you fa *(fah)*

doctor medico/a *(meh-dee-koh/-kah)*

dog cane, il *(kah-nay)*

door porta, la *(pohr-tah)*

double bed letto matrimoniale, il *(leht-toh mah-tree-mohn-nyah-lay)*

double room camera doppia, la *(kah-may-rah dohp-pyah)*

downtown centro, il *(chehn-troh cheet-tah)*

down giù *(joo)*

dress vestito, il *(vays-tee-toh)*

dried beans fagioli, i *(fahd-joh-lee)*

drink, to bere *(bay-ray)*

drink, safe to potabile *(poh-tah-bee-lay)*

drink, not safe to non potabile *(nohn poh-tah-bee-lay)*

drinks bevande *(bay-vahn-day)*

drive, to (e.g., a car) guidare *(gwee-dah-ray)*

drive, I guido *(gwee-doh)*

drive, we guidiamo *(gwee-dyah-moh)*

drive, you guida *(gwee-dah)*

driver's license patente (di guida), la *(pah-tehn-tay [dee gwee-dah])*

drugstore (medicine) farmacia, la *(fahr-mah-chee-ah)*; (sundry items) negozio di generi vari, il *(nay-goht-tsyoh dee jehn-ay-ree vah-ree)*

dumpling gnocco di pasta, lo *(nyohk-koh dee pah-stah)*

ear orecchio, l' *m (oh-rayk-kyoh)*

early presto *(preh-stoh)*

east, to the all'est *(ahl-ehst)*

eat, to mangiare *(mahn-jah-ray)*

eat, I mangio *(mahn-joh)*

eat, we mangiamo *(mahn-jah-moh)*

eat, you mangia *(mahn-jah)*

egg uovo, l' *m (woh-voh)*

eight otto *(oht-toh)*

eight hundred ottocento *(oh-toh-chehn-toh)*

eighteen diciotto *(dee-choht-toh)*

eighty ottanta *(oht-tahn-tah)*

elbow gomito, il *(goh-mee-toh)*

eleven undici *(oon-dee-chee)*

engineer ingegnere, l' *m (een-jayn-nyeh-ray)*

England Inghilterra, l' *f (een-geel-teh-rah)*

English inglese *(een-glay-say)*

enough abbastanza *(ahb-bahs-tahn-tsah)*

entrance ingresso, l' *m (een-grehs-soh)*; entrata, l' *f (ayn-trah-tah)*

entry entrata, l' *(ayn-trah-tah)*

error errore, l' *m (ayr-roh-ray)*

espresso espresso, l' *m (ays-prehs-soh)*

euro euro, l' *m (ay-oo-roh)*

evening sera, la *(say-rah)*

evening, in the di sera *(dee say-rah)*

exchange, to cambiare *(kahm-byah-ray)*

exchange office ufficio di cambio, l' *m (oof-fee-choh dee kahm-byoh)*

excuse me (mi) scusi *([mee] skoo-zee)*; (="May I get past") permesso? *(payr-mays-soh?)*

exit uscita, l' *f (oosh-shee-tah)*

expensive caro/a *(kah-roh/-rah)*

extra supplemento/a *(soo-play-mayn-toh/-tah)*

eye occhio, l' *m (ohk-kyoh)*

eyeglasses occhiali, gli *(ohk-kyah-lee)*

face viso, il *(vee-zoh)*; la faccia *(faht-chah)*

facial tissues fazzoletti di carta, i *(faht-tsoh-layt-tee dee kahr-tah)*

fall (season) autunno, l' *m (aw-toon-noh)*

family famiglia, la *(fah-meel-lyah)*

far away lontano *(lohn-tah-noh)*

farmer agricoltore, l' *m (ah-gree-kohl-toh-ray)*

father padre, il *(pah-dray)*

Father's Day festa del papà, la *(feh-stah dayl pah-pah)*

February febbraio *(fayb-brah-yoh)*

ferry traghetto, il *(trah-gayt-toh)*

fever febbre, la *(fehb-bray)*

fewer meno *(may-noh)*

fifteen quindici *(kween-dee-chee)*

fifty cinquanta *(cheen-kwahn-tah)*

fill up the tank "Il pieno, per favore" *(eel pyeh-noh, payr fah-voh-ray)*

film, roll of rollino, il *(rohl-lee-noh)*

finger dito, il *(dee-toh)*

fire! Al fuoco! *(ahl foo-oh-koh)*

firemen pompieri, i *(pohm-pyeh-ree)*

fish pesce, il *(paysh-shay)*

five cinque *(cheenk-way)*

five hundred cinquecento *(cheen-kway-chehn-toh)*

fixed-price meal menù a prezzo fisso, il *(may-noo ah preht-tsoh fees-soh)*

flight volo, il *(voh-loh)*

floor (of room) pavimento, il *(pah-vee-mayn-toh)*; (story of building) piano, il *(pyah-noh)*

foggy nebbioso/a *(nayb-byoh-soh/-sah)*

food, traditional cucina tradizionale, la *(koo-chee-nah trah-deet-tsyoh-nah-lay)*

foot piede, il *(pyeh-day)*

for per *(payr)*

forbidden vietato/a *(vyay-tah-toh/-tah)*

foreign straniero/a *(strah-nyeh-roh/-rah)*

fork forchetta, la *(fohr-kayt-tah)*

fortress fortezza, la *(fohr-tayt-tsah)*

forty quaranta *(kwah-rahn-tah)*

fountain fontana, la *(fohn-tah-nah)*

four quattro *(kwaht-troh)*

four hundred quattrocento *(kwaht-troh-chehn-toh)*

fourteen quattordici *(kwaht-tohr-dee-chee)*

fowl pollame, il *(pohl-lah-may)*

France Francia, la *(frahn-chah)*

free (no cost) gratuito/a *(grah-too-ee-toh/-tah)*; (available) libero/a *(lee-bay-roh/-rah)*

fresh fresco/a *(fray-skoh/-skah)*

French fries patate fritte *(pah-tah-tay freet-tay)*; patatine *(pah-tah-tee-nay)*

Friday venerdì *(vay-nayr-dee)*

friend (male) amico, l' *m (ah-mee-koh)*; (female) amica, l' *f (ah-mee-kah)*

from da *(dah)*

from. . . until da. . . a *(dah. . . ah)*

fruit frutta, la *(froot-tah)*

fruit juice succo di frutta, il *(sook-koh dee froo-tah)*

full completo/a *(kohm-pleh-toh/-tah)*

game, wild selvaggina, la *(sayl-vahd-jee-nah)*

garden giardino, il *(jahr-dee-noh)*

gasoline benzina, la *(bayn-dzee-nah)*

gas station stazione di servizio, la *(stah-tsyoh-nay dee sayr-veet-tsyoh)*

gentlemen's room signori *(seen-nyoh-ree)*

Germany Germania, la *(jayr-mahn-yah)*

gift shop negozio di regali, il *(nay-goht-tsyoh dee ray-gah-lee)*

girl ragazza, la *(rah-gaht-tsah)*

girlfriend ragazza, la *(rah-gaht-tsah)*

glass bicchiere, il *(beek-kyeh-ray)*

glasses occhiali, gli *(ohk-kyah-lee)*

gloves guanti, i *(gwahn-tee)*

go! vada *(vah-dah)*

go away! Se ne vada! *(say nay vah-dah)*

go, to andare *(ahn-dah-ray)*

go, I vado *(vah-doh)*

go, we andiamo *(ahn-dyah-moh)*

go, you va *(vah)*

God dio, il *(dee-oh)*

god-awful orrendo/a *(ohr-rohn-doh/-dah)*

golden (color) dorato/a *(doh-rah-toh)*

good buono/a *(bwohn-oh/-ah)*

goodbye arrivederci *(ahr-ree-vay-dayr-chee)*

good day! Buon giorno! *(bwohn johr-noh)*

good evening! Buona sera! *(bwohn-ah say-rah)*

good morning! Buon giorno! *(bwohn johr-noh)*

good night! Buona notte! *(bwohn-ah noht-tay)*

grandchildren nipoti (di nonni), i *(nee-poh-tay)*

granddaughter nipote, la (di nonni) *(nee-poh-tay)*

grandfather nonno, il *(nohn-noh)*

grandmother nonna, la *(nohn-nah)*

grandparents nonni, i *(nohn-nee)*

grandson nipote, il (di nonni) *(nee-poh-tay)*

grape uva, l' f *(oo-vah)*

grapefruit pompelmo, il *(pohm-pehl-moh)*

gray grigio/a *(gree-joh/-jah)*

green verde *(vayr-day)*

green beans fagiolini, i *(fahd-joh-lee-nee)*

grocery store drogheria, la *(droh-gay-ree-ah)*; negozio di alimentari, il *(nay-goht-tsyoh dee ah-lee-mayn-tah-ree)*

guesthouse pensione, la *(payn-syoh-nay)*

hairdresser parrucchiere, il *(pahr-rook-kyeh-ray)*; la parrucchiera *(pahr-rook-kyeh-rah)*

half mezzo/a *(mehd-dzoh/-dzah)*

ham prosciutto, il *(prohsh-shoot-toh)*

hamburger hamburger, l' *(ahm-boor-gayr)*

hand mano, la *(mah-noh)*

handbag borsetta, la *(bohr-sayt-tah)*

hard duro/a *(doo-roh/-rah)*

hat cappello, il *(kahp-pehl-loh)*

have, to avere *(ah-vay-ray)*

have, I ho *(oh)*

have, you ha *(ah)*

have, we abbiamo *(ahb-byah-moh)*

he lui *(loo-ee)*

head testa, la *(teh-stah)*

headache mal di testa, il *(mahl dee teh-stah)*

heart cuore, il *(kwoh-ray)*

heart condition disturbi cardiaci, i *(dees-toor-bee kahr-dee-ah-chee)*

heating riscaldamento, il *(rees-kahl-dah-mayn-toh)*

hello buon giorno *(bwohn johr-noh)*; ciao *(chow)*

help, to aiutare *(ah-yoo-tah-ray)*

help! aiuto! *(ah-yoo-toh)*

here qui *(kwee)*

here is ecco *(chk-koh)*

hi ciao *(chow)*

high alto/a *(ahl-toh/-tah)*

high blood pressure pressione alta, la *(prays-syoh-nay ahl-tah)*

highway autostrada, l' f *(ow-tohs-trah-dah)*

historical center centro storico, il *(chehn-troh stoh-ree-koh)*

honey miele, il *(myeh-lay)*

hospital ospedale, l' m *(ohs-pay-dah-lay)*

hot caldo/a *(kahl-doh/-dah)*

hot chocolate cioccolata calda, la *(choh-koh-lah-tah kahl-dah)*

hot dog hot dog, l'

hotel albergo, l' m *(ahl-behr-goh)*

hour ora, l' f *(oh-rah)*

hours of business orario di apertura, l' m *(oh-rahr-yoh dee ah-payr-too-rah)*

housewife casalinga, la *(kah-sah-leen-gah)*

house wine vino della casa, il *(vee-noh dayl-lah kah-sah)*

how come *(koh-may)*

how long quanto *(kwahn-toh)*; (=how long will something take) quanto dura *(kwahn-toh doo-rah)*

how many quanti *(kwahn-tee)*; quante (fem.) *(kwahn-tay)*

how much quanto *(kwahn-toh)*

hundred cento *(chehn-toh)*

hurt dolore, il *(doh-loh-ray)*

hurts here, it mi fa male qui *(mee fah mah-lay kwee)*

husband marito, il *(mah-ree-toh)*

I io *(yoh)*

ice ghiaccio, il *(gyaht-choh)*

ice cream gelato, il *(jay-lah-toh)*

ice cubes cubetti di ghiaccio, i *(koo-bayt-tee dee gyaht-choh)*

include, to includere *(een-kloo-day-ray)*

included incluse *(een-kloo-day)*; incluso *(een-kloo-soh)*

identity card carta d'identità, la *(kahr-tah dee dayn-tee-tah)*

immediately subito *(soo-bee-toh)*

in in *(een)*

information informazioni *(een-fohr-maht-tsyoh-nee)*

inn locanda, la *(loh-kahn-dah)*

insurance assicurazione, l' *f (ahs-see-koo-raht-tsyoh-nay)*

is è *(eh)*

it (subject) esso/a *(ays-soh/-sah)*; (direct object) lo/la/l' *(loh/lah/l)*

Italian Italiano *(ee-tah-lyah-noh)*

Italy Italia, l' *f (ee-tahl-yah)*

jacket giacca, la *(jahk-kah)*

jam marmellata, la *(mahr-mayl-lah-tah)*

January gennaio *(jayn-nah-yoh)*

jeans jeans, i *(jeenz)*

juice succo, il *(sook-koh)*

July luglio *(lool-lyoh)*

June giugno *(joon-nyoh)*

just a moment un momento *(oon moh-mayn-toh)*

ketchup ketchup, il *(kay-choop)*

key chiave, la *(kyah-vay)*

knee ginocchio, il *(jee-nohk-kyoh)*

knife coltello, il *(kohl-tehl-loh)*

laborer manovale, il *(mah-noh-vah-lay)*

lady signora, la *(seen-nyoh-rah)*

ladies' room signore *(seen-nyoh-ray)*

lamb agnello, l' *m (ahn-nyehl-loh)*

lamp lampada, la *(lahm-pah-dah)*

lasagna lasagne *(lah-zahn-nyay)*

late tardi *(tahr-dee)*

lawyer avvocato *(ahv-voh-kah-toh)*

left sinistra *(see-nee-strah)*

leg gamba, la *(gahm-bah)*

lemon limone, il *(lee-moh-nay)*

lemonade limonata, la *(lee-moh-nah-tah)*

less meno *(may-noh)*

letter lettera, la *(leht-tay-rah)*

lettuce lattuga, la *(laht-too-gah)*

lettuce, red radicchio, il *(rah-deek-kyoh)*

light luce, la *(loo-chay)*

light colored chiaro/a *(kyah-roh/-rah)*

lighter (cigarette) accendino, l' *m (aht-chayn-dee-noh)*

like (it), I mi piace *(mee pyah-chay)*

like (them), I mi piacciono *(mee pyaht-choh-noh)*

like, I would vorrei *(vohr-reh-ee)*; desidero *(day-zee-day-roh)*

like, we would vorremmo *(vohr-rehm-moh)*; desideriamo *(day-zee-dayr-yah-moh)*

like, you would desidera *(day-zee-dayr-ah)*

liquor store enoteca, l' *f (ay-noh-teh-kah)*

liter litro, il *(lee-troh)*

little piccolo/a *(peek-koh-loh/-lah)*

little (of), a un po' (di) *(oon poh [dee])*

liver fegato, il *(fay-gah-toh)*

locker, luggage deposito bagagli automatico, il *(day-poh-zee-toh bah-gahl-lyee ow-toh-mah-tee-koh)*

long lungo/a *(loon-goh/-gah)*

look, to guardare *(gwahr-dah-ray)*

look, I guardo *(gwahr-doh)*

look, we guardiamo *(gwahr-dyah-moh)*

look, you guarda *(gwahr-dah)*

look for, to cercare *(chayr-kah-ray)*

look for, I cerco *(chayr-koh)*

look for, we cerchiamo *(chayr-kyah-moh)*

look for, you cerca *(chayr-kah)*

looking guardando *(gwahr-dahn-doh)*

Look out! attenzione! *(aht-tayn-tsyoh-nay)*

lot, a molto *(mohl-toh)*

loud/loudly forte *(fohr-tay)*

louder/more loudly più forte *(pyoo fohr-tay)*

luggage bagaglio, il *(bah-gahl-lyoh)*

luggage checkroom deposito bagagli, il *(day-poh-zee-toh bah-gahl-lyee)*

luggage locker deposito bagagli automatico, il *(day-poh-zee-toh bah-gahl-lyee ow-toh-mah-tee-koh)*

lunch pranzo, il *(prahn-dzoh)*

magazine rivista, la *(ree-vees-tah)*

mail posta, la *(pohs-tah)*

mailbox cassetta delle lettere, la *(kahs-sayt-tah dayl-lay leht-tay-ray)*

main square piazza principale, la *(pyaht-tsah preen-chee-pah-lay)*

man uomo, l' *m (woh-moh)*

manager direttore, il *(dee-rayt-toh-ray)*

map mappa, la *(mahp-pah)*; carta, la *(kahr-tah)*

March marzo *(mahr-tsoh)*

market mercato, il *(mayr-kah-toh)*

married sposato/a *(spoh-zah-toh/-tah)*

match fiammifero, il *(fyahm-mee-fay-roh)*

may (=be able to) potere *(poh-<u>tay</u>-ray)*

may I?/I may posso *(<u>pohs</u>-soh)*

may you/you may possa *(<u>pohs</u>-sah)*

may we/we may possiamo *(pohs-<u>syah</u>-moh)*

May maggio *(<u>mahj</u>-joh)*

maybe forse *(<u>fohr</u>-say)*

mayonnaise maionese, la *(mah-yoh-<u>nay</u>-say)*

meal pasto, il *(<u>pahs</u>-toh)*

meat carne, la *(<u>kahr</u>-nay)*

meatball polpetta di carne, la *(pohl-<u>payt</u>-tah dee <u>kahr</u>-nay)*

meat dish piatto di carne, il *(<u>pyah</u>-toh dee <u>kahr</u>-nay)*

mechanic meccanico, il *(mayk-<u>kah</u>-nee-koh)*

medication medicinali, i *(may-dee-chee-<u>nah</u>-lee)*

medicine medicina, la *(may-dee-<u>chee</u>-nah)*

medium (cooked meat) a puntino *(ah poon-<u>tee</u>-noh)*; (size) regolare *(ray-goh-<u>lah</u>-ray)*

men's room uomo *(<u>woh</u>-moh)*

menu menù, il *(may-<u>noo</u>)*

middle (of place) di mezzo *(dee <u>mehd</u>-dzoh)*, centrale *(chayn-<u>trah</u>-lay)*; in size/quality) medio/a *(<u>mehd</u>-yoh/-yah)*

midnight mezzanotte, la *(mayd-dzah-<u>noht</u>-tay)*

mild dolce *(<u>dohl</u>-chay)*

milk latte, il *(<u>laht</u>-tay)*

million milione, il *(mee-<u>lyoh</u>-nay)*

mineral water acqua minerale, l' *f (<u>ahk</u>-kwah mee-nay-<u>rah</u>-lay)*

minister pastore, il *(pahs-<u>toh</u>-ray)*

minus meno *(<u>may</u>-noh)*

minute minuto, il *(mee-<u>noo</u>-toh)*

miss (young woman) signorina, la *(seen-nyoh-<u>ree</u>-nah)*

mistake errore, l' *m (ayr-<u>roh</u>-ray)*

moment, just a un momento *(oon moh-<u>mayn</u>-toh)*

Monday lunedì *(loo-nay-<u>dee</u>)*

money denaro, il *(day-<u>nah</u>-roh)*; soldi, i *(<u>sohl</u>-dee)*

month mese, il *(<u>may</u>-say)*

more più *(pyoo)*

morning mattina, la *(maht-<u>tee</u>-nah)*

morning, in the di mattina *(dee maht-<u>tee</u>-nah)*

mother madre, la *(<u>mah</u>-dray)*

Mother's Day festa della mamma, la *(<u>fehs</u>-tah <u>dayl</u>-lah <u>mahm</u>-mah)*

motorcycle motocicletta, la *(moh-toh-chee-<u>klayt</u>-tah)*

mouth bocca, la *(<u>bohk</u>-kah)*

much molto/a *(<u>mohl</u>-toh/-tah)*

museum museo, il *(moo-<u>zeh</u>-oh)*

mushrooms funghi, i *(<u>foon</u>-gee)*

musician musicista, il/la *(moo-zee-<u>chee</u>-stah)*

mustard senape, la *(<u>seh</u>-nah-pay)*; mostarda, la *(mohs-<u>tahr</u>-dah)*

my mio/a *(<u>mee</u>-oh/-ah)*

name nome, il *(<u>noh</u>-may)*

napkin tovagliolo, il *(toh-vahl-<u>lyoh</u>-loh)*

nearby vicino *(vee-<u>chee</u>-noh)*

neck collo, il *(<u>kohl</u>-loh)*

necktie cravatta, la *(krah-<u>vaht</u>-tah)*

need bisogno, il *(bee-<u>zohn</u>-yoh)*

nephew nipote (di zii), il *(nee-<u>poh</u>-tay)*

newspaper giornale, il *(johr-<u>nah</u>-lay)*

newstand edicola, l' *f (ay-<u>dee</u>-koh-lah)*

nice bello/a *(behl-<u>loh</u>/-lah)*

niece nipote (di zii), la *(nee-<u>poh</u>-tay)*

night notte, la *(<u>noht</u>-tay)*

night, at di notte *(dee <u>noht</u>-tay)*

nine nove *(<u>noh</u>-vay)*

nine hundred novecento *(noh-vay-<u>chehn</u>-toh)*

nineteen dicannove *(dee-chahn-<u>noh</u>-vay)*

ninety novanta *(noh-<u>vahn</u>-tah)*

no no *(noh)*

noisy rumoroso/a *(roo-moh-<u>roh</u>-soh/sah)*

non-carbonated naturale *(nah-too-<u>rah</u>-lay)*

noon mezzogiorno, il *(mayd-dzoh-<u>johr</u>-noh)*

north (of), (to the) (a) nord (di) *([ah] nohrd [dee])*

nose naso, il *(<u>nah</u>-soh)*

not non *(nohn)*

November novembre *(noh-<u>vehm</u>-bray)*

number numero, il *(<u>noo</u>-may-roh)*

nun suora, la *(<u>swoh</u>-rah)*

nurse infermiere/a, l'/l' *m/f (een-fayr-<u>myeh</u>-ray/-rah)*

nuts frutta secca, la *(<u>froot</u>-tah <u>sayk</u>-kah)*

occupied occupato/a *(ohk-koo-<u>pah</u>-toh/-tah)*

October ottobre *(oht-<u>toh</u>-bray)*

octopus polipo, il *(<u>poh</u>-lee-poh)*

of di *(dee)*

oil olio, l' *m* (*ohl*-yoh)

OK, that's va bene (vah *beh*-nay)

old vecchio/a (*vayk*-kyoh/-kyah)

old part of town parte vecchia della
città, la (*pahr*-tay *vayk*-kyah *dayl*-lah
cheet-*tah*)

olive oliva, l' *f* (oh-*lee*-vah)

olive oil olio d'oliva, l' *m* (*ohl*-yoh doh-
lee-vah)

omelette frittata, la (*freet*-*tah*-tah);
omeletta, l' *f* (oh-muh-*leht*-tah);
omelette, l' *f* (oh-muh-*leht*)

on su (soo); sopra (*soh*-prah)

one uno (*oo*-noh)

one-way (traffic) a senso unico (ah
sehn-soh *oo*-nee-koh); (ticket) di sola
andata (dee *soh*-lah ahn-*dah*-tah)

onion cipolla, la (chee-*pohl*-lah)

only solo/a (*soh*-loh/-lah)

open (to be) aperto/a (ah-*pehr*-toh/-tah)

or o (oh)

orange (fruit) arancia, l' *f* (ah-*rahn*-
chah); (color) arancione (ah-rahn-*choh*-
nay)

order, to place an ordinare (ohr-dee-
nah-ray)

our nostro/a (*nohs*-troh/-trah)

outside fuori (*fwoh*-ree)

overcoat cappotto, il (kahp-*poht*-toh)

palace palazzo, il (pah-*laht*-tsoh)

pants, pair of pantaloni, i (pahn-tah-*loh*-
nee)

paper carta, la (*kahr*-tah)

paper, toilet carta igienica, la (*kahr*-tah
ee-*jeh*-nee-kah)

pardon me! mi scusi! (mee *skoo*-zee)

parents genitori, i (jay-nee-*toh*-ree)

park parco, il (*pahr*-koh)

parking disk disco orario, il (*dees*-koh
oh-*rahr*-yoh)

parking lot parcheggio, il (pahr-*kayd*-
joh)

parking meter parchimetro, il (pahr-
kee-may-troh)

passport passaporto, il (pahs-sah-*pohr*-
toh)

passport control controllo
passaporti, il (kohn-*trohl*-loh pahs-sah-
pohr-tee)

pasta pasta, la (*pah*-stah)

pastry shop pasticceria, la (pahs-teet-
chay-*ree*-ah)

pay, to pagare (pah-*gah*-ray)

pay attention! attenzione! (aht-tayn-
tsyoh-nay)

peach pesca, la (*pehs*-kah)

pear pera, la (*pay*-rah)

peas piselli (pee-*sehl*-lee)

pen, ballpoint penna, la (*payn*-nah)

penicillin penicillina, la (pay-nee-cheel-
lee-nah)

person persona, la (payr-*soh*-nah)

people persone, le (payr-*soh*-nay)

pepper pepe, il (*pay*-pay)

perfume profumo, il (proh-*foo*-moh)

perfumery profumeria, la (proh-foo-
may-*ree*-ah)

person persona, la (payr-*soh*-nah)

pet animale domestico, l' *m* (ah-nee-
mah-lay doh-*mehs*-tee-koh)

pharmacy farmacia, la (fahr-mah-*chee*-
ah)

photo shop negozio di fotocine, il
(nay-*goht*-tsyoh dee foh-toh-*chee*-nay)

pictures, to take fotografare (foh-toh-
grah-*fah*-ray)

pink rosa (*roh*-sah)

pizzeria pizzeria, la (peet-tsay-*ree*-ah)

plate piatto, il (*pyaht*-toh)

platform (train station) binario, il
(bee-*nahr*-yoh)

please per favore (payr fah-*voh*-ray); per
piacere (payr pyah-*chay*-ray)

plumber idraulico, l' *m* (ee-*draw*-lee-
koh)

p.m. (afternoon) del pomeriggio (dayl
poh-may-*reed*-joh); (evening) di sera (dee
say-rah)

police polizia, la (poh-leet-*tsee*-ah)

pop bibita frizzante, la (bee-*bee*-tah freed-
zahn-tay)

pork maiale, il (mah-*yah*-lay)

portion porzione, la (pohr-*tsyoh*-nay)

portions, children's porzioni per (i)
bambini, le (pohr-*tsyoh*-nay payr [ee]
bahm-*bee*-nee)

postage stamp francobollo, il (frahn-
koh-*bohl*-loh)

postcard cartolina, la (kahr-toh-*lee*-nah)

post office ufficio postale, l' *m* (oof-
fee-choh pohs-*tah*-lay)

potato patata, la (pah-*tah*-tah)

poultry pollame, il (pohl-*lah*-may)

prawns gamberi, i (*gahm*-bay-ree)

prescription ricetta, la (ree-*cheht*-tah)

press, to spingere (*speen*-jay-ray)

pretty bello/a (*behl*-loh/-lah)

priest   prete, il *(preh-tay)*
professor   professore/essa, il/la *(proh-fays-soh-ray/-rays-sah)*
prohibited   vietato/a *(vyay-tah-toh/-tah)*
pudding   budino, il *(boo-dee-noh)*
pull, to   tirare *(tee-rah-ray)*
pullover   maglione, il *(mahl-lyoh-nay)*
purple   viola *(vee-oh-lah)*
purse   borsetta, la *(bohr-sayt-tah)*
push, to   spingere *(speen-jay-ray)*
quiet   tranquillo/a *(trahn-kweel-loh/-lah)*
quarter   quarto *(kwahr-toh)*
rabbit   coniglio, il *(koh-neel-lyoh)*
raining, it's   piove *(pyoh-vay)*
rare   (cooked meat) al sangue *(ahl sahn-gway)*
rare, very   (cooked meat) quasi crudo/a *(kwah-zee kroo-doh/-dah)*
raspberry   lampone, il *(lahm-pohn-nay)*
raw   crudo/a *(kroo-doh/-dah)*
razor blades   lamette da barba, le *(lah-mayt-tay dah bahr-bah)*
ready   pronto/a *(prohn-toh/-tah)*
receipt   ricevuta, la *(ree-chay-voo-tah)*; (when prepaying) scontrino, lo *(skohn-tree-noh)*
recommend, to   consigliare *(kohn-seel-lyah-ray)*
red   rosso/a *(rohs-soh/-sah)*
red wine   vino rosso, il *(vee-noh rohs-soh)*
rent, to   noleggiare *(noh-layd-jah-ray)*
repeat, to   ripetere *(ree-peh-tay-ray)*
reservation   prenotazione, la *(pray-noh-tah-tsyoh-nay)*
restaurant   ristorante, il *(ree-stoh-rahn-tay)*
retired   in pensione *(een payn-syoh-nay)*
rice   riso, il *(ree-soh)*
right   destra *(deh-strah)*
right away   subito *(soo-bee-toh)*
roll   panino, il *(pah-nee-noh)*
room   camera, la *(kah-may-rah)*
rooster   gallo, il *(gahl-loh)*
round trip   andata e ritorno *(ahn-dah-tah ay ree-tohr-noh)*
salad   insalata, l' *f (een-sah-lah-tah)*
salad, mixed   insalata mista, l' *f (een-sah-lah-tah mees-tah)*
sales   saldi *(sahl-dee)*
salesperson   commesso/a, il/la *(kohm-mays-soh/-sah)*

sales representative   rappresentante di commercio, il/la *(rahp-pray-zayn-tahn-tay dee kohm-mehrt-choh)*
sales tax   L'IVA *(lee-vah)*
salmon   salmone, il *(sahl-moh-nay)*
salt   sale, il *(sah-lay)*
sandals   sandali, i *(sahn-dah-lee)*
Saturday   sabato *(sah-bah-toh)*
sauce   salsa, la *(sahl-sah)*
sausages   salsicce, le *(sahl-see-chay)*
scientist   scienziato/a, lo/la *(shayn-tsyah-toh/-tah)*
seafood   frutti di mare, i *(froot-tee dee mah-ray)*
seafood chowder   cacciucco, il *(kaht-chook-koh)*
second   secondo, il *(say-kohn-doh)*
secretary   segretario/a, il/la *(say-gray-tahr-yoh/-yah)*
see   vedere *(vay-day-ray)*
self-employed, I'm   Lavoro in proprio *(lah-voh-roh een proh-pyoh)*
self-service station   distributore automatico, il *(dee-stree-boo-toh-ray ow-toh-mah-tee-koh)*
separate/separated   separato/a *(say-pah-rah-toh/-tah)*
separately   separatamente *(say pah rah tah-mayn-tay)*
September   settembre *(sayt-tehm-bray)*
service   servizio, il *(sayr-veet-tsyoh)*
set-priced meal   menù a prezzo fisso, il *(may-noo ah preht-tsoh fees-soh)*
seven   sette *(seht-tay)*
seven hundred   settecento *(say-tay-chehn-toh)*
seventeen   diciassette *(dee-chas-seht-tay)*
seventy   settanta *(sayt-tahn-tah)*
shampoo   shampoo, lo *(shahm-poo)*
sharp   (flavor) piccante *(peek-kahn-tay)*
shaving cream   crema da barba, la *(kreh-mah dah bahr-bah)*
shirt   camicia, la *(kah-mee-chah)*
shoe   scarpa, la *(skahr-pah)*
shorts   shorts, gli *(shoorts)*
shoulder   spalla, la *(spahl-lah)*
shower   doccia, la *(doht-chah)*
sick, I'm   Mi sento male *(mee sayn-toh may-lay)*
silver   (metal) argento, l' *m (ahr-jehn-toh)*; (color) argenteo/a *(ahr-jehn-tay-oh/-ah)*
simple   semplice *(saym-plee-chay)*

single singolo/a *(seen-goh-loh/-lah)*;
(man) celibe *(cheh-lee-bay)*;
(woman) nubile *(noo-bee-lay)*

single room camera singola, la *(kah-may-rah seen-goh-lah)*

sister sorella, la *(soh-rehl-lah)*

six sei *(seh-ee)*

six hundred seicento *(say-ee-chehn-toh)*

sixteen sedici *(say-dee-chee)*

sixty sessanta *(says-sahn-tah)*

skin pelle, la *(pehl-lay)*

skirt gonna, la *(gohn-nah)*

slice fetta, la *(fayt-tah)*

slow/slowly lentamente *(layn-tah-mayn-tay)*

small piccolo/a *(peek-koh-loh/-lah)*

smoking fumare *(foo-mah-ray)*; fumo *(foo-moh)*

snack spuntino, lo *(spoon-tee-noh)*

snack bar snack-bar, lo; tavola calda/fredda, la *(tah-voh-lah kahl-dah/frayd-dah)*

snowing, it's nevica *(nay-vee-kah)*

soap, bar of saponetta, la *(sah-poh-nayt-tah)*

socks calzini, i *(kahl-tsee-nee)*

soda pop bibita frizzante, la *(bee-bee-tah freed-zahn-tay)*

soft molle *(mohl-lay)*

soft drink bibita frizzante, la *(bee-bee-tah freed-zahn-tay)*

something qualcosa *(kwahl-koh-sah)*

son figlio, il *(feel-lyoh)*

sorry, I'm mi dispiace *(mee dees-pyah-chay)*

soup zuppa, la *(tsoo-pah)*

soup of the day zuppa del giorno, la *(tsoo-pah dayl johr-noh)*

sour acido/a *(ah-chee-doh/-dah)*

south (of), (to the) (a) sud (di) *([ah] sood [dee])*

spaghetti spaghetti, gli *(spah-gayt-tee)*

Spain Spagna, la *(spahn-nyah)*

speak, to parlare *(pahr-lahr-ay)*

speak? do you parla? *(pahr-lah)*

speak, I parlo *(pahr-loh)*

special offer offerta speciale, l' *f (ohf-fehr-tah spay-chah-lay)*

spinach spinaci, gli *(spee-nah-chee)*

spoon cucchiaio, il *(kook-kyah-yoh)*

spring primavera, la *(pree-mah-veh-rah)*

square piazza, la *(pyaht-tsah)*

stadium stadio, lo *(stah-dyoh)*

stamp francobollo, il *(frahn-koh-boh-loh)*

steak bistecca, la *(bee-stayk-kah)*

stew stufato, lo *(stoo-fah-toh)*

stomach stomaco, lo *(stoh-mah-koh)*

stomach ache mal di stomaco, il *(mah dee stoh-mah-koh)*

stop! fermo! *(fayr-moh)*

store/shop negozio, il *(nay-goht-tsyoh)*

straight (alcohol) liscio *(lee-shoh)*

straight ahead dritto *(dreet-toh)*

strawberry fragola, la *(frah-goh-lah)*

streetcar tram, il *(trahm)*

student studente/essa, lo/la *(stoo-dehn-tay/-tays-sah)*

subway metropolitana, la *(may-troh-poh-lee-tah-nah)*; metro, il *(may-troh)*

sugar zucchero, lo *(tsoo-kay-roh)*

suitcase valigia, la *(vah-leej-jah)*

summer estate, l' *f (ays-tah-tay)*

Sunday domenica, la *(doh-may-nee-kah)*

sunglasses occhiali da sole, gli *(oh-kyah-lee dah soh-lay)*

sunny, it's c'è il sole *(chay eel soh-lay)*

sunscreen crema solare protettiva, la *(kreh-mah soh-lah-ray proh-tayt-tee-vah)*

suntan cream crema solare, la *(kreh-mah soh-lah-ray)*

suntan oil olio solare, l' *m (ohl-yoh soh-lah-ray)*

sun umbrella ombrellone, l' *m (ohm-brayl-loh-nay)*

supermarket supermercato, il *(soo-payr-mayr-kah-toh)*

supplementary supplemento/a *(soo-play-mayn-toh/-tah)*

supper cena, la *(chay-nah)*

sweater maglione, il *(mahl-lyoh-nay)*

sweatshirt felpa, la *(fayl-pah)*

sweet dolce *(dohl-chay)*

Switzerland Svizzera, la *(zveet-tsay-rah)*

table tavola, la *(tah-voh-lah)*

take, to prendere *(prehn-day-ray)*

take, you prenda *(prehn-dah)*

take it, I'll lo/la prendo *(loh/lah prehn-doh)*

tap water acqua del rubinetto, l' *f (ahk-kwah dayl roo-bee-nayt-toh)*

tastes good/bad, it ha un buon/cattivo sapore *(ah oon bwohn/kaht-tee-voh sah-poh-ray)*

taxi taxi, il *(tahk-see)*; tassì, il *(tahs-see)*

tea tè, il *(tay)*

teacher insegnante, l' *m/f* *(een-sayn-nyahn-tay)*

telephone telefono, il *(tay-leh-foh-noh)*

ten dieci *(dyeh-chee)*

terrible terribile *(tayr-ree-bee-lay)*

terrific fantastico/a *(fahn-tahs-tee-koh/-kah)*

thank you (very much) (mille) grazie *([meel-lay] graht-tsyay)*

that (thing) quello/a *(kway-loh/-lah)*

that's all è tutto *(ay toot-toh)*

then poi *(poy)*

there là *(lah)*

there are ecco! *(ehk-koh) [= here (they) are!]*; ci sono *(chee soh-noh) [= there are, there exist]*

there is ecco! *(ehk-koh) [= here (it) is!]*; c'è *(chay) [= there is, there exists]*

thing cosa, la *(koh-sah)*

thirteen tredici *(tray-dee-chee)*

thirty trenta *(trayn-tah)*

this questo *(kway-stoh)*

thousand mille *(meel-lay)*

three tre *(tray)*

three hundred trecento *(tray-chehn-toh)*

throat gola, la *(goh-lah)*

Thursday giovedì *(joh-vay-dee)*

ticket biglietto, il *(beel-lyayt-toh)*

tie cravatta, la *(krah-vaht-tah)*

time tempo, il *(tehm-poh)*

tip mancia, la *(mahn-chah)*

tire pneumatico, lo *(pnay-oo-mah-tee-koh)*

tissues, facial fazzoletti di carta, i *(faht-tsoh-layt-tee dee kahr-tah)*

to a *(ah)*

toast pane tostato, il *(pah-nay toh-stah-toh)*

tobacconist's shop tabaccheria, la *(tah-bahk-kay-ree-ah)*

today oggi *(oh-jee)*

together (as in the bill) unico/a *(oo-nee-koh/-kah)*

toilet toilette, la *(twah-leht)*; toeletta, la *(toh-ay-leht-tah)*

toilet paper carta igienica, la *(kahr-tah ee-jeh-nee-kah)*

toll (on road) pedaggio, il *(pay-dahd-joh)*

tomato pomodoro, il *(poh-moh-doh-roh)*

tomorrow domani *(doo-mah-nee)*

tomorrow, day after dopodomani *(doh-poh-doh-mah-nee)*

tonight questa notte *(kways-tah noht-tay)*; stasera *(stah-say-rah)*

tonsils tonsille, le *(tohn-seel-lay)*

too troppo *(trohp-poh)*; (=also) anche *(ahn-kay)*

tooth dente, il *(dehn-tah)*

toothpaste dentifricio, il *(dayn-tee-free-choh)*

touch, to toccare *(tohk-kah-ray)*

touch!, don't non toccare! *(nohn tohk-kah-ray)*

tourist turista, il/la *(too-rees-tah)*

tourist information office ufficio turistico, l' *m* *(oof-fee-choh too-rees-tee-koh)*

town hall municipio, il *(moo-nee-chee-pyoh)*

town square piazza principale, la *(pyaht-tsah preen-chee-pah-lay)*

traffic jam ingorgo (del traffico), l' *m* *(een-gohr-goh [dayl trahf-fee-koh])*

train treno, il *(treh-noh)*

train platform binario, il *(bee-nahr-yoh)*

train station stazione ferroviaria, la *(staht-tsyoh-nay fayr-roh-vyah-ryah)*

train ticket biglietto, il *(beel-lyayt-toh)*

train track binario, il *(bee-nahr-yoh)*

tram tram, il *(trahm)*

traveler's check assegno turistico, l' *m* *(ahs-sayn-nyoh too-ree-stee-koh)*

trip viaggio, il *(vee-ahd-joh)*

trout trota, la *(troh-tah)*

T-shirt T-shirt, la *(tee-shirt)*

Tuesday martedì *(mahr-tay-dee)*

tuna tonno, il *(tohn-noh)*

turkey tacchino, il *(tahk-kee-noh)*

twelve dodici *(doh-dee-chee)*

twenty venti *(vayn-tee)*

twin beds due letti *(doo-ay leht-tee)*

two due *(doo-ay)*

two hundred duecento *(doo-ay-chehn-toh)*

umbrella ombrello, l' *m* *(ohm-brehl-loh)*

uncle zio, lo *(tsee-oh)*

under sotto *(soht-toh)*

underpants mutande, le *(moo-tahn-day)*

understand, to capire *(kah-pee-ray)*

understand, I capisco *(kah-pees-koh)*

understand, I don't non capisco *(nohn kah-pees-koh)*

underwear, pair of mutande, le *(moo-tahn-day)*

unemployed disoccupato/a *(deez-ohk-koo-pah-toh/-tah)*

United States, the Stati Uniti, gli *(stah-tee oo-nee-tee)*

until a *(ah)*

up su *(soo)*

USA U.S.A. *(oo-zah)*

vacant libero/a *(lee-bay-roh/-rah)*

vanilla vaniglia *(vah-neel-lyah)*

veal vitello, il *(vee-tehl-loh)*

vegetables verdure, le *(vayr-doo-ray)*

vegetables, mixed verdura mista , la *(vayr-doo-rah mees-tah)*

vegetable soup minestrone, il *(mee-nay-stroh-nay)*

vegetarian restaurant ristorante vegetariano, il *(ree-stoh-rahn-tay vay-jay-tah-ryah-noh)*

vinegar aceto, l' *m* *(ah-chay-toh)*

waiter/waitress cameriere/a *(kah-may-ree-eh-ray/-rah)*

waiter! cameriere! *(kah-may-ree-eh-ray)*; signore! *(seen-nyoh-ray)*

waitress! cameriera! *(kah-may-ree-eh-rah)*; signora! *(seen-nyoh-rah)*

wall muro, il *m* *(moo-roh)*

warm caldo/a *(kahl-doh/-dah)*

was (it) era *(eh-rah)*; (I) ero *(eh-roh)*

wastebasket cestino per la cartaccia, il *(chays-tee-noh payr lah kahr-taht-chah)*

Watch out! attenzione! *(ah-tayn-tsyoh-nay)*

water acqua, l' *f* *(ahk-kwah)*

waterbus vaporetto, il *(vah-poh-rayt-toh)*

we noi *(noy)*

weak debole *(day-boh-lay)*

weather tempo, il *(tehm-poh)*

Wednesday mercoledì *(mayr-koh-lay-dee)*

week settimana, la *(sayt-tee-mah-nah)*

weekend fine settimana, il *(fee-nay sayt-tee-mah-nah)*

welcome, you're prego *(preh-goh)*

well bene *(beh-nay)*

well done/well cooked (cooked meat) ben cotto/a *(behn koht-toh/-tah)*

west (of), (to the) (a) ovest (di) *([ah] oh-vayst [dee])*

what che cosa *(kay koh-sah)*; che *(kay)*; quale *(kwah-lay)*

what is that? che cos'è quello? *(kay koh-say kwayl-loh?)*

wheel ruota, la *(rwoh-tah)*

when quando *(kwahn-doh)*

where dove *(doh-vey)*

where from da dove *(dah doh-vey)*

where is dov'è *(doh-veh)*

whipped cream panna montata, la *(pahn-nah mohn-tah-tah)*

white bianco/a *(byahn-koh/-kah)*

white wine vino bianco, il *(vee-noh byahn-koh)*

who chi *(kee)*

why perché *(payr-kay)*

widowed vedovo/a *(vay-doh-voh/-vah)*

wife moglie, la *(mohl-lyay)*

window finestra, la *(fee-neh-strah)*

windy ventoso/a *(vayn-toh-soh/-sah)*

windy, it's tira vento *(tee-rah vehn-toh)*

wine vino, il *(vee-noh)*

wine, house vino della casa, il *(vee-noh dayl-lah kah-sah)*

wine list lista dei vini, la *(lee-stah day-ee vee-nee)*

winter inverno, l' *m* *(een-vehr-noh)*

with con

without senza *(sehn-tsah)*

woman donna, la *(dohn-nah)*

would like, I vorrei *(vohr-reh-ee)*; desidero *(day-zee-day-roh)*

would like, we vorremmo *(vohr-rehm-moh)*; desideriamo *(day-zee-dayr-yah-moh)*

wristwatch orologio da polso, l' *m* *(oh-roh-loh-joh dah pohl-soh)*

write, to scrivere *(skree-vay-ray)*

write it, please lo scriva, per favore *(loh skree-vah, payr fah-voh-ray)*

writing paper carta da lettere, la *(kahr-tah dah leht-tay-ray)*

year anno, l' *m* *(ahn-noh)*

yellow giallo/a *(jahl-loh/-lah)*

yes sì *(see)*

yesterday ieri *(yeh-ree)*

you lei *(leh-ee)*

you're welcome prego *(preh-goh)*

zero zero *(dzeh-roh)*

Index

Notes

Notes

Order Form

Italian Survival Guide: The Language and Culture You Need to Travel with Confidence in Italy. 192-page paperback book.

German Survival Guide: The Language and Culture You Need to Travel with Confidence in Germany and Austria. 192-page paperback book.

See www.worldprospect.com for the latest list of products.

Shipping Information—*Please print clearly.*

Name _____

Address _____

City/State/Zip _____

Day phone _____

E-mail address _____

U.S. shipping and handling: $3 first item, $1 each additional item

_____ *Italian Survival Guide*, book	x	$19.95	$	_____
_____ *German Survival Guide*, book	x	$19.95	$	_____
		Subtotal:	$	_____
Iowa addresses add 7% sales tax			$	_____
__1__ Shipping, 1st item*	x	$3.00	$	3.00
_____ Shipping, additional items	x	$1.00	$	_____
_____ Priority mail		add $3 per order	$	_____
		Order Total	$	_____

* Allow 2-3 weeks for delivery

Send with check to:
World Prospect Press, PO Box 100, Shell Rock, IA 50670

Survival Summary
Part Two

Transportation

taxi	il taxi	*tahk-see*
to __	a __	*ah __*
I get off here.	Scendo qui.	*shayn-doh kwee*
city bus	l'autobus	*ow-toh-boos*
rural bus	il pullman	*pool-mahn*
entrance	l'ingresso	*een-grehs-soh*
exit	l'uscita	*oosh-shee-tah*
subway	il metro	*may-troh*
train	il treno	*treh-noh*
train platform	il binario	*bee-nahr-yoh*
ticket	il biglietto	*beel-lyayt-toh*
car	l'auto	*ow-toh*
I would like to rent a car.	Vorrei noleggiare un'auto.	*vohr-reh-ee noh-layd-jah-ray oon ow-toh*
I have a reservation.	Ho una prenotazione.	*oh oon-ah pray-noh-taht-tsyoh-nay*
from . . . to	da . . . a	*dah . . . ah*
driver's license	la patente (di guida)	*pah-tehn-tay (dee gwee-dah)*
plane flight	il volo	*voh-loh*
airport	l'aeroporto	*ay-roh-pohr-toh*
information	informazioni	*een-fohr-maht-tsyoh-nee*

Services

bathroom	la toilette	*twah-leht*
gentlemen	signori	*seen-nyoh-ree*
ladies	signore	*seen-nyoh-ray*
available	libero/a	*lee-bay-roh/-rah*
occupied	occupato/a	*ohk-koo-pah-toh/-tah*
ATM	il bancomat	*bahn-koh-maht*
bank	la banca	*bahn-kah*
telephone	il telefono	*tay-leh-foh-noh*
post office	l'ufficio postale	*oof-fee-choh pohs-stah-lay*
stamps	francobolli	*frahn-koh-boh-lee*
to America	a America	*ah ah-may-ree-kah*
by airmail	per via aerea	*payr vee-ah ah-eh-ray-ah*

Temperature Conversion Guide

1. Multiply the Celsius reading by 2.
2. Add 30, for approximate Fahrenheit temperature.

Numbers

0	zero	*dzeh-roh*
1	uno	*oo-noh*
2	due	*doo-ay*
3	tre	*tray*
4	quattro	*kwaht-troh*
5	cinque	*cheen-kway*
6	sei	*seh-ee*
7	sette	*seht-tay*
8	otto	*oht-toh*
9	nove	*noh-vay*
10	dieci	*dyeh-chee*
11	undici	*oon-dee-chee*
12	dodici	*doh-dee-chee*
13	tredici	*tray-dee-chee*
14	quattordici	*kwaht-tohr-dee-chee*
15	quindici	*kween-dee-chee*
16	sedici	*say-dee-chee*
17	diciassette	*dee-chah-seht-tay*
18	diciotto	*dee-choht-toh*
19	diciannove	*dee-chahn-noh-vay*
20	venti	*vayn-tee*
21	ventuno	*vayn-too-noh*
22	ventidue	*vayn-tee-doo-ay*
33	trentatré	*trayn-tah-tray*
44	quaranta-quattro	*kwah-rahn-tah-kwaht-troh*
55	cinquanta-cinque	*cheen-kwahn-tah-cheen-kway*
66	sessantasei	*says-sahn-tah-seh-ee*
77	settantasette	*sayt-tahn-tah-seht-tay*
88	ottantotto	*oht-tahn-toht-toh*
99	novantanove	*noh-vahn-tah-noh-vay*
100	cento	*chehn-toh*
101	centouno	*chayn-toh-oo-noh*
102	centodue	*chayn-toh-doo-ay*
200	duecento	*doo-ay-chehn-toh*
300	trecento	*tray-chehn-toh*
400	quattrocento	*kwaht-troh-chehn-toh*
500	cinquecento	*cheen-kway-chehn-toh*
600	seicento	*say-ee-chehn-toh*
700	settecento	*say-tay-chehn-toh*
800	ottocento	*oht-toh-chehn-toh*
900	novecento	*noh-vay-chehn-toh*
1.000	mille	*meel-lay*
2.000	duemila	*doo-ay-mee-lah*